baking

100 **everyday** recipes

First published in 2011
LOVE FOOD is an imprint of Parragon Books Ltd

Parragon
Queen Street House
4 Queen Street
Bath BA1 1HE, UK

ISBN: 978-1-4454-3047-8

Printed in China

Created by Ivy Contract
Photography by Charlie Paul

Notes for the Reader

This book uses imperial, metric, or US cup measurements. Follow the same units of measurement throughout; do not mix imperial and metric. All spoon measurements are level: teaspoons are assumed to be 5 ml, and tablespoons are assumed to be 15 ml. Unless otherwise stated, milk is assumed to be full fat, eggs and individual vegetables, such as potatoes, are medium, and pepper is freshly ground black pepper.

The times given are an approximate guide only. Preparation times differ according to the techniques used by different people and the cooking times may also vary from those given. Optional ingredients, variations, or serving suggestions have not been included in the calculations.

Recipes using raw or very lightly cooked eggs should be avoided by infants, the elderly, pregnant women, convalescents, and anyone with a chronic condition. Pregnant and breast-feeding women are advised to avoid eating peanuts and peanut products. People with nut allergies should be aware that some of the prepared ingredients used in the recipes in this book may contain nuts. Always check the package before use.

baking

introduction

Baking is without any doubt the most rewarding of culinary experiences. To mix together the most unpromising-looking collection of ingredients, put them in an oven, and have them emerge as a truly delicious creation is nothing short of a miracle!

No wonder, then, that there is something of a mystery to the whole process that is often daunting to an inexperienced cook. In reality, however, it's nowhere near as difficult as it might appear to bake a sumptuous large cake, a melt-in-the-mouth muffin, your favorite pie, a loaf of bread to serve fresh from the oven, or an elegant savory tart—and these are just a few examples of the wonderful baking recipes you will find in this book.

There are several items of kitchen equipment that are worth investing in if you are planning to make baking a regular event. A selection of baking pans is a must—cookie sheets and tart pans, as well as round and square cake pans of various sizes, including one or two of the "springform" type to facilitate the removal of large cakes, tortes, and cheesecakes.

Apart from this, a couple of generously sized mixing bowls, some wooden spoons, and perhaps a hand-held electric mixer will be enough to get you started. A more expensive item of equipment that will pay for itself in no time is a multipurpose food mixer. The different attachments will enable you to mix cake batters and pie doughs, whisk egg whites, whip cream, and knead bread dough with speed and efficiency. In the past, of course, cooks had no such gadgets to help them out, and there is a certain satisfaction in doing all of the above tasks by hand—kneading bread dough for ten minutes is guaranteed to relieve tension as well as produce a fabulous result.

Choose your favorite recipe, mix it together with confidence—and wait for the golden moment when you can bite into it!

cakes & gâteaux

coffee & walnut cake

ingredients

serves 8

6 oz/175 g butter, plus
    extra for greasing
6 oz/175 g/¼ cup light brown
    sugar
3 extra-large eggs, beaten
3 tbsp strong black coffee
6 oz/175 g/1½ cups self-rising
    flour
1½ tsp baking powder
1 cup walnut pieces
walnut halves, to decorate

frosting

4 oz/115 g butter
7 oz/200 g/1¾ cups confectioners'
    sugar
1 tbsp strong black coffee
½ tsp vanilla extract

method

1 Grease and line the bottoms of two 8-inch/20-cm round layer cake pans.

2 Cream together the butter and brown sugar until pale and fluffy. Gradually add the eggs, beating well after each addition. Beat in the coffee.

3 Sift the flour and baking powder into the mixture, then fold in lightly and evenly with a metal spoon. Fold in the walnut pieces.

4 Divide the batter between the prepared cake pans and smooth level. Bake in a preheated oven, 350°F/180°C, for 20–25 minutes, or until golden brown and springy to the touch. Turn out onto a wire rack to cool.

5 For the frosting, beat together the butter, confectioners' sugar, coffee, and vanilla extract, mixing until smooth and creamy.

6 Use about half of the frosting to sandwich the cakes together, then spread the remaining frosting on top and swirl with a metal spatula. Decorate with walnut halves.

hummingbird cake

ingredients

serves 10

scant 1 cup sunflower oil,
plus extra for greasing

9 oz/250 g/2¼ cups all-purpose
flour

9 oz/250 g/1¼ cups superfine
sugar

1 tsp ground cinnamon

1 tsp baking soda

3 eggs, beaten

3½ oz/100 g/scant 1 cup pecans,
coarsely chopped, plus extra
to decorate

3 oz/85 g/1 cup mashed ripe
bananas (about 3 bananas)

3 oz/85 g canned crushed
pineapple (drained weight),
plus 4 tbsp juice from the can

frosting

6 oz/175 g/¾ cup cream cheese

2 oz/55 g unsalted butter

1 tsp vanilla extract

14 oz/400 g/3½ cups confectioners'
sugar

method

1 Lightly grease three 9-inch/23-cm layer cake pans with
oil and line the bottoms with parchment paper.

2 Sift together the flour, superfine sugar, cinnamon,
and baking soda into a large bowl. Add the eggs, oil,
pecans, bananas, and pineapple with the juice and
stir with a wooden spoon until evenly mixed.

3 Divide the batter among the prepared pans, spreading
it evenly. Bake in a preheated oven, 350°F/180°C,
for 25–30 minutes, or until golden brown and firm
to the touch.

4 Remove the cakes from the oven and let cool for
10 minutes in the pans before turning out onto
wire racks to cool.

5 For the frosting, beat together the cream cheese,
butter, and vanilla extract in a bowl until smooth.
Sift in the confectioners' sugar and mix until smooth.

6 Sandwich the cakes together with half of the frosting,
spread the remaining frosting over the top, then
sprinkle with pecans to decorate.

pound cake

ingredients

serves 8–10

6 oz/175 g unsalted butter,
    plus extra for greasing
6 oz/175 g scant 1 cup superfine
    sugar
finely grated rind of 1 lemon
3 extra-large eggs, beaten
4 oz/115 g/1 cup all-purpose flour
4 oz/115 g/1 cup self-rising flour
2–3 tbsp brandy or milk
2 slices of citron peel

method

1 Grease and line a 7-inch/18-cm round deep cake pan.

2 Cream together the butter and sugar until pale and fluffy. Add the lemon rind and gradually beat in the eggs. Sift in the flours and fold in evenly, adding enough brandy to make a soft consistency.

3 Spoon the batter into the prepared pan and smooth the surface. Lay the slices of citron peel on top of the cake.

4 Bake in a preheated oven, 325°F/160°C for 1–1¼ hours, or until well risen, golden brown, and springy to the touch.

5 Cool in the pan for 10 minutes, then turn out and cool completely on a wire rack.

red velvet cake

ingredients

serves 12

8 oz/225 g unsalted butter,
   plus extra for greasing
4 tbsp water
2 oz/55 g/½ cup unsweetened
   cocoa
3 eggs
9 fl oz/250 ml/generous 1 cup
   buttermilk
2 tsp vanilla extract
2 tbsp red edible food coloring
10 oz/280 g/2½ cups all-purpose
   flour
2 oz/55 g/½ cup cornstarch
1½ tsp baking powder
10 oz/280 g/scant 1½ cups
   superfine sugar

frosting

9 oz/250 g/generous 1 cup
   cream cheese
3 tbsp unsalted butter
3 tbsp superfine sugar
1 tsp vanilla extract

method

1 Grease two 9-inch/23-cm layer cake pans and line the bottoms with parchment paper. Place the butter, water, and cocoa in a small saucepan and heat gently, without boiling, stirring until melted and smooth. Remove from the heat and let cool slightly.

2 Beat together the eggs, buttermilk, vanilla extract, and food coloring until frothy. Beat in the butter mixture. Sift together the flour, cornstarch, and baking powder, then stir into the mixture with the superfine sugar.

3 Divide the batter between the prepared pans and bake in a preheated oven, 375°F/190°C, for 25–30 minutes, or until risen and firm to the touch. Cool in the pans for 3–4 minutes, then turn out and finish cooling on a wire rack.

4 For the frosting, beat together all the ingredients until smooth. Use about half of the frosting to sandwich the cakes together, then spread the remainder over the top, swirling with a metal spatula.

variation

If you prefer not to use food coloring, use 4 tablespoons of beet juice mixed with 2 tablespoons of water. With an electric juicer, 1 medium beet should yield about 4 tablespoons of juice.

orange & poppy seed bundt cake

ingredients

serves 10

9 oz/250 g unsalted butter,
    plus extra for greasing
7 oz/200 g/1 cup superfine sugar
3 extra-large eggs, beaten
finely grated rind of 1 orange
2 oz/55 g/¹/₂ cup poppy seeds
10¹/₂ oz/300 g/2¹/₄ cups all-purpose
    flour, plus extra for dusting
2 tsp baking powder
5 fl oz/150 ml/²/₃ cup milk
4 fl oz/125 ml/¹/₂ cup orange juice
strips of orange zest, to decorate

syrup

5 oz/140 g/scant ³/₄ cup superfine
    sugar
5 fl oz/150 ml/²/₃ cup orange juice

method

1 Grease and lightly flour a Bundt ring pan, about
  9¹/₂ inches/24 cm in diameter and with a capacity of
  approximately 8³/₄ cups.

2 Cream together the butter and sugar until pale and
  fluffy, then add the eggs gradually, beating thoroughly
  after each addition. Stir in the orange rind and poppy
  seeds. Sift in the flour and baking powder, then fold
  in evenly.

3 Add the milk and orange juice, stirring to mix evenly.
  Spoon the batter into the prepared pan and bake in
  a preheated oven, 325°F/160°C, for 45–50 minutes,
  or until firm and golden brown. Cool in the pan for
  10 minutes, then turn out onto a wire rack to cool.

4 For the syrup, place the sugar and orange juice in a
  saucepan and heat gently until the sugar melts. Bring
  to a boil and simmer for about 5 minutes, until reduced
  and syrupy.

5 Spoon the syrup over the cake while it is still warm. Top
  with the strips of orange zest and serve warm or cold.

birthday lemon sponge cake

ingredients

serves 8–10

sponge
9 oz/250g unsalted butter,
    plus extra for greasing
9 oz/250 g/1¼ cups superfine
    sugar
4 eggs, beaten
9 oz/250 g/2¼ cups self-rising
    flour
finely grated rind of 1 lemon
3 tbsp milk

butter frosting
5 oz/140 g unsalted butter
7 oz/200g confectioners' sugar
2 tbsp lemon juice or lemon
    liqueur (Limoncello)
3 tbsp lemon curd

method

1 Grease two 8-inch/20-cm layer cake pans and line the bottoms with parchment paper.

2 Cream together the butter and superfine sugar until pale and fluffy. Gradually add the eggs, beating well after each addition. Sift in the flour and fold in evenly with a metal spoon. Fold in the lemon rind and milk lightly and evenly.

3 Spoon the batter into the prepared pans and bake in the preheated oven, 350°F/180°C, for 25–30 minutes, or until golden brown and springy to the touch. Let the cakes cool in the pans for 2–3 minutes, then turn out onto a wire rack to finish cooling.

4 For the butter frosting, beat together the butter, confectioners' sugar, and lemon juice until smooth. Mix about 3 tablespoons of the butter cream with the lemon curd. Use the lemon curd mixture to sandwich together the two cakes.

5 Spread about two thirds of the remaining butter frosting over the top of the cake, swirling with a spatula. Spoon the remainder into a pastry bag and pipe swirls around the edge of the cake. Add candleholders and birthday candles to finish.

chocolate fudge cake

ingredients

serves 8

6 oz/175 g unsalted butter,
    softened, plus extra
    for greasing
6 oz/175 g/scant 1 cup golden
    superfine sugar
3 eggs, beaten
3 tbsp dark corn syrup
1½ oz/40 g/⅓ cup ground almonds
6 oz/175 g/1¼ cups self-rising
    flour
pinch of salt
1½ oz/40 g/⅓ cup unsweetened
    cocoa

frosting

8 oz/225 g plain chocolate,
    broken into pieces
2 oz/55 g/⅓ cup dark
    muscovado sugar
8 oz/225 g unsalted butter, diced
5 tbsp evaporated milk
½ tsp vanilla extract

method

1 Grease and line the bottom of 2 x 8-inch/20-cm round cake pans. To make the frosting, place the chocolate, sugar, butter, evaporated milk, and vanilla extract in a heavy-bottom pan. Heat gently, stirring constantly, until melted. Pour into a bowl and let cool. Cover and let chill in the refrigerator for 1 hour, or until spreadable.

2 Place the butter and sugar in a bowl and beat together until light and fluffy. Gradually beat in the eggs. Stir in the syrup and ground almonds. Sift the flour, salt, and cocoa into a separate bowl, then fold into the mixture. Add a little water, if necessary, to make a dropping consistency. Spoon the mixture into the prepared pans and bake in a preheated oven, 350°F/180°C, for 30–35 minutes, or until springy to the touch and a skewer inserted in the center comes out clean.

3 Leave the cakes in the pans for 5 minutes, then turn out onto wire racks to cool completely. When the cakes are cold, sandwich them together with half the frosting. Spread the remaining frosting over the top and sides of the cake, swirling it to give a frosted appearance.

carrot cake

ingredients

serves 16

2 eggs

6 oz/175 g/¾ cup molasses sugar

7 fl oz/200 ml/scant 1 cup
   sunflower oil

7 oz/200 g/generous 1⅓ cups
   coarsely grated carrots

8 oz/225 g/2 cups all-purpose
   whole-wheat flour

1 tsp baking soda

2 tsp ground cinnamon

whole nutmeg, grated
   (about 1 tsp)

4 oz/115 g/1 cup roughly
   chopped walnuts

topping

4 oz/115 g/½ cup half-fat
   cream cheese

4 tbsp butter, softened

3 oz/85 g/¾ cup confectioners'
   sugar

1 tsp grated lemon rind

1 tsp grated orange rind

strips of lemon and orange zest,
   to decorate

method

1 In a mixing bowl, beat the eggs until well blended
   and add the sugar and oil. Mix well. Add the grated
   carrot, sift in the flour, baking soda, and spices, then
   add the walnuts. Mix everything together until well
   incorporated.

2 Spread the mixture into the prepared cake pan and
   bake in the center of a preheated oven, 375°F/190°C,
   for 40–50 minutes until the cake is nicely risen, firm to
   the touch, and has begun to shrink away slightly from
   the edge of the pan. Remove from the oven and let
   cool in the pan until just warm, then turn out onto
   a wire rack.

3 To make the topping, put all the ingredients into
   a mixing bowl and beat together for 2–3 minutes
   until really smooth.

4 When the cake is completely cold, spread with the
   topping, smooth over with a fork. Decorate with
   orange and lemon zest and let firm up a little before
   cutting into 16 portions. Store in an airtight container
   in a cool place for up to 1 week.

sponge cake

ingredients

serves 8–10

6 oz/175 g butter, at room
 temperature
6 oz/175 g/¾ cup superfine sugar
3 eggs, beaten
6 oz/175 g/scant 1¼ cups
 self-rising flour
pinch of salt

to serve

3 tbsp raspberry jelly
1 tbsp superfine or confectioners'
 sugar, to serve

method

1 Grease 2 x 8-inch/20-cm round layer cake pans and
 base-line with parchment paper.

2 Beat the butter and sugar together in a mixing bowl
 using a wooden spoon or a hand-held mixer until the
 mixture is pale in color and light and fluffy. Add the
 egg, a little at a time, beating well after each addition.

3 Sift the flour and salt and carefully add to the mixture,
 folding it in with a metal spoon or a spatula. Divide the
 mixture among the pans and smooth over with the
 spatula. Place them on the same shelf in the center
 of a preheated oven, 350°F/180°C, and bake for 25–30
 minutes until well risen, golden brown and beginning
 to shrink from the sides of the pan.

4 Remove from the oven and let stand for 1 minute.
 Loosen the cakes from around the edge of the pans
 using a round-bladed knife. Turn the cakes out onto a
 clean dish towel, remove the paper and invert them
 onto a wire rack (this prevents the wire rack from
 marking the top of the cakes). When completely cool,
 sandwich together with the jelly and sprinkle
 with the sugar.

sticky ginger marmalade loaf

ingredients

serves 10

6 oz/175 g butter, softened,
    plus extra for greasing
4½ oz/125 g/⅓ cup ginger
    marmalade
6 oz/175 g/scant 1 cup
    brown sugar
3 eggs, beaten
8 oz/225 g/generous
    1½ cups self-rising flour
½ tsp baking powder
1 tsp ground ginger
3½ oz/100 g/⅔ cup coarsely
    chopped pecans

method

1 Grease and line the bottom and ends of a 2-lb/900-g loaf pan. Place 1 tablespoon of the ginger marmalade in a small pan and reserve. Place the remaining marmalade in a bowl with the butter, sugar, and eggs.

2 Sift in the flour, baking powder, and ground ginger and beat together until smooth. Stir in three-fourths of the nuts. Spoon the mixture into the prepared loaf pan and smooth the top. Sprinkle with the remaining nuts and bake in a preheated oven, 350°F/180°C, for 1 hour, or until well risen and a skewer inserted into the center comes out clean.

3 Let cool in the pan for 10 minutes, then turn out and peel off the lining paper. Transfer to a wire rack to cool until warm. Set the pan of reserved marmalade over low heat to warm, then brush over the loaf and serve in slices.

variation

For something different, replace the coarsely chopped pecans with 3½ oz/100 g coarsely chopped macadamia nuts or walnuts.

date & walnut loaf

ingredients

serves 10

6 oz/175 g butter, plus extra
    for greasing
8 oz/225 g/scant 1⅓ cups
    pitted dates, chopped into
    small pieces
grated rind and juice
    of 1 orange
2 fl oz/50 ml/scant ¼ cup water
6 oz/175g/scant 1 cup
    brown sugar
3 eggs, beaten
3 oz/85 g/⅔ cup self-rising
    whole-wheat flour
3 oz/85 g/⅔ cup self-rising flour
2 oz/55 g/½ cup chopped walnuts
8 walnut halves
orange zest, to decorate

method

1 Grease and line the bottom and ends of a 2-lb/900-g loaf pan. Place the dates in a pan with the orange rind and juice and water and cook over medium heat for 5 minutes, stirring, or until a soft puree has formed.

2 Place the butter and sugar in a bowl and beat together until light and fluffy. Gradually beat in the eggs, then sift in the flours and fold in with the chopped walnuts. Spread one third of the mixture over the bottom of the prepared loaf pan and spread half the date puree over the top.

3 Repeat the layers, ending with the cake mixture. Arrange walnut halves on top. Bake in a preheated oven, 325°F/160°C, for 1–1¼ hours, or until well risen and firm to the touch. Let cool in the pan for 10 minutes. Turn out, peel off the lining paper, and transfer to a wire rack to cool. Decorate with orange zest and serve in slices.

gingerbread

ingredients

serves 12–16

1 lb/450 g/3½ cups
all-purpose flour
3 tsp baking powder
1 tsp baking soda
3 tsp ground ginger
6 oz/175 g butter
6 oz/175 g/¾ cup soft
brown sugar
6 oz/175 g/½ cup black molasses
6 oz/175 g/½ cup dark corn syrup
1 egg, beaten
10 fl oz/300 ml/1¼ cups milk

method

1 Line a 9-inch/23-cm square cake pan, 2 inches/5 cm deep, with parchment paper.

2 Sift the flour, baking powder, baking soda, and ginger into a large mixing bowl.

3 Place the butter, sugar, molasses, and syrup in a medium pan and heat over low heat until the butter has melted and the sugar dissolved. Let cool a little.

4 Mix the beaten egg with the milk and add to the cooled syrup mixture. Add the liquid ingredients to the flour mixture and beat well using a wooden spoon until the mixture is smooth and glossy.

5 Pour the mixture into the prepared pan and bake in the center of a preheated oven, 325°F/160°C, for 1½ hours until well risen and just firm to the touch.

6 Remove from the oven and let cool in the pan. When cool, remove the cake from the pan, with the lining paper. Overwrap with foil and place in an airtight container for up to 1 week to allow the flavors to mature. Cut into wedges to serve.

torta de cielo

ingredients

serves 6–8

8 oz/225g/1 cup unsalted butter,
    at room temperature,
    plus extra for greasing
6 oz/175 g/1¼ cups whole
    almonds, in their skins
8 oz/225 g/1¼ cups sugar
3 eggs, lightly beaten
1 tsp almond extract
1 tsp vanilla extract
9 tbsp all-purpose flour
pinch of salt

to decorate

confectioners' sugar, for dusting
slivered almonds, toasted

method

1 Lightly grease an 8-inch/20-cm round cake pan and
line the pan with parchment paper.

2 Place the almonds in a food processor and process
to form a "mealy" mixture. Set aside.

3 Beat the butter and sugar together in a large bowl
until smooth and fluffy. Beat in the eggs, almonds,
and both the almond and vanilla extracts until well
blended. Stir in the flour and salt and mix briefly, until
the flour is just incorporated.

4 Pour or spoon the batter into the prepared pan and
smooth the surface. Bake in a preheated oven, 350°F/
180°C, for 40–50 minutes, or until the cake feels spongy
when gently pressed.

5 Remove from the oven and let stand on a wire rack
to cool. To serve, dust with confectioners' sugar and
decorate with toasted slivered almonds.

chocolate truffle torte

ingredients

serves 10

butter, for greasing
2 oz/55 g/generous ¼ cup golden
    superfine sugar
2 eggs
1 oz/25 g/scant ¼ cup
    all-purpose flour
1 oz/25 g/¼ cup unsweetened
    cocoa, plus extra to decorate
2 fl oz/50 ml/¼ cup cold strong
    black coffee
2 tbsp brandy

topping

20 fl oz/600 ml/2½ cups heavy
    cream
15 oz/425 g semisweet chocolate,
    melted and cooled
confectioners' sugar, to decorate

method

1 Grease a 9-inch/23-cm springform cake pan with butter
  and line the bottom with parchment paper. Place the
  sugar and eggs in a heatproof bowl and set over a pan
  of hot water. Whisk together until pale and mousse-like.
  Sift the flour and unsweetened cocoa into a separate
  bowl, then fold gently into the cake batter. Pour into
  the prepared pan and bake in a preheated oven,
  425°F/220°C, for 7–10 minutes, or until risen and firm
  to the touch.

2 Transfer to a wire rack to cool. Wash and dry the pan
  and put the cooled cake back in the pan. Mix the
  coffee and brandy together and brush over the cake.

3 To make the topping, place the cream in a bowl and
  whip until very soft peaks form. Carefully fold in the
  cooled chocolate. Pour the chocolate mixture over the
  sponge and let chill in the refrigerator for 4–5 hours,
  or until set.

4 To decorate the torte, sift unsweetened cocoa over the
  top and remove carefully from the pan. Using strips of
  card or waxed paper, sift bands of confectioners' sugar
  over the torte to create a striped pattern. To serve, cut
  into slices with a hot knife.

moroccan orange & almond cake

ingredients

serves 8

1 orange
4 oz/115 g butter, softened,
    plus extra for greasing
4 oz/115 g/generous ½ cup golden
    superfine sugar
2 eggs, beaten
6 oz/175 g/scant 1 cup semolina
3½ oz/100 g/generous 1 cup
    ground almonds
1½ tsp baking powder
confectioners' sugar, for dusting
strained plain yogurt, to serve

syrup

10 fl oz/300 ml/1¼ cups
    orange juice
4¼ oz/130 g/⅔ cup superfine sugar
8 cardamom pods, crushed

method

1 Grate the rind from the orange, reserving some for the decoration, and squeeze the juice from one half. Place the butter, orange rind, and sugar in a bowl and beat together until light and fluffy. Beat in the eggs.

2 In a separate bowl, mix the semolina, ground almonds, and baking powder, then fold into the creamed mixture with the orange juice. Spoon the batter into a greased and base-lined 8-inch/20-cm cake pan and bake in a preheated oven, 350°F/180°C, for 30–40 minutes, or until well risen and a skewer inserted into the center comes out clean. Let cool in the pan for 10 minutes.

3 To make the syrup, place the orange juice, sugar, and cardamom pods in a pan over low heat and stir until the sugar has dissolved. Bring to a boil and let simmer for 4 minutes, or until syrupy.

4 Turn the cake out into a deep serving dish. Using a skewer, make holes over the surface of the warm cake. Strain the syrup into a separate bowl and spoon three-fourths of it over the cake, then let stand for 30 minutes. Dust the cake with confectioners' sugar and cut into slices. Serve with the remaining syrup drizzled around, accompanied by strained plain yogurt decorated with the reserved orange rind.

caribbean coconut cake

ingredients

serves 8

10 oz/280 g butter, softened,
plus extra for greasing
6 oz/175 g/scant 1 cup golden
superfine sugar
3 eggs
6 oz/175 g/1¼ cups self-rising
flour
1½ tsp baking powder
½ tsp freshly grated nutmeg
2 oz/55 g/⅔ cup dry
unsweetened coconut
5 tbsp coconut cream
10 oz/280 g/2¼ cups
confectioners' sugar
5 tbsp pineapple jelly
dry unsweetened coconut, toasted,
to decorate

method

1 Grease and base-line 2 x 8-inch/20-cm layer cake pans. Place 6 oz/175 g of the butter in a bowl with the sugar and eggs and sift in the flour, baking powder, and nutmeg. Beat together until smooth, then stir the coconut and 2 tablespoons of the coconut cream into the mixture.

2 Divide the mixture among the prepared pans and smooth the tops. Bake in a preheated oven, 350°F/180°C, for 25 minutes, or until golden and firm to the touch. Let cool in the pans for 5 minutes, then turn out onto a wire rack, peel off the lining paper, and let cool completely.

3 Sift the confectioners' sugar into a bowl and add the remaining butter and coconut cream. Beat together until smooth. Spread the pineapple jelly on one of the cakes and top with just under half of the buttercream. Place the other cake on top. Spread the remaining buttercream on top of the cake and scatter with the toasted coconut.

honey spiced cake

ingredients

serves 8

5½ oz/150 g butter, plus extra
   for greasing
4 oz/115 g/generous ½ cup
   brown sugar
6 oz/175 g/½ cup honey
1 tbsp water
7 oz/200 g/scant 1½ cups
   self-rising flour
½ tsp ground ginger
½ tsp ground cinnamon
½ tsp caraway seeds
seeds from 8 cardamom pods,
   ground
2 eggs, beaten
12 oz/350 g/3½ cups
   confectioners' sugar

method

1 Grease a 28-fl oz/875-ml/3½-cup fluted cake pan.
   Place the butter, sugar, honey, and water into a heavy-
   bottom pan. Set over low heat and stir until the butter
   has melted and the sugar has dissolved. Remove from
   the heat and let cool for 10 minutes.

2 Sift the flour into a bowl and mix in the ginger,
   cinnamon, caraway seeds, and cardamom. Make a well
   in the center. Pour in the honey mixture and the eggs
   and beat well until smooth. Pour the batter into the
   prepared pan and bake in a preheated oven, 350°F/
   180°C, for 40–50 minutes, or until well risen and a
   skewer inserted into the center comes out clean. Let
   cool in the pan for 5 minutes, then transfer to a wire
   rack to cool completely.

3 Sift the confectioners' sugar into a bowl. Stir in enough
   warm water to make a smooth, flowing frosting.
   Spoon over the cake, allowing it to flow down the
   sides, then let set.

rich fruit cake

ingredients

serves 8

butter, for greasing
6 oz/175 g/1 cup pitted
    unsweetened dates
4½ oz/125 g/¾ cup no-soak
    dried prunes
7 fl oz/200 ml/scant 1 cup
    unsweetened orange juice
2 tbsp molasses
1 tsp finely grated lemon rind
1 tsp finely grated orange rind
8 oz/225 g/generous 1½ cups
    whole-wheat self-rising flour
1 tsp pumpkin pie spice
4½ oz/125 g/¾ cup seedless raisins
4½ oz/125 g/¾ cup golden raisins
4½ oz/125 g/¾ cup currants
4½ oz/125 g/¾ cup dried cranberries
3 large eggs, separated
1 tbsp apricot jelly, warmed

frosting

4½ oz/125 g/generous 1 cup
    confectioners' sugar
1–2 tsp water
1 tsp vanilla extract
orange and lemon zest, to decorate

method

1 Grease and line a deep 8-inch/20-cm round cake pan.
   Chop the dates and prunes and place in a pan. Pour
   over the orange juice and let simmer for 10 minutes.
   Remove the pan from the heat and beat the fruit
   mixture until puréed. Add the molasses and citrus
   rind and let cool.

2 Sift the flour and spice into a bowl, adding any bran
   that remains in the sifter. Add the dried fruits. When the
   date and prune mixture is cool, whisk in the egg yolks.
   Whisk the egg whites in a separate, clean bowl until
   stiff. Spoon the fruit mixture into the dry ingredients
   and mix together.

3 Gently fold in the egg whites. Transfer to the prepared
   pan and bake in a preheated oven, 325°F/160°C, for
   1½ hours. Let cool in the pan.

4 Remove the cake from the pan and brush the top with
   jelly. To make the frosting, sift the sugar into a bowl
   and mix with enough water and the vanilla extract to
   form a soft frosting. Lay the frosting over the top of the
   cake and trim the edges. Decorate with orange and
   lemon zest.

chocolate cherry gâteau

ingredients

serves 10

3 tbsp unsalted butter, melted, plus extra for greasing

2 lb/900 g fresh cherries, pitted and halved

9 oz/250 g/generous 1¼ cups superfine sugar

3½ fl oz/100 ml/scant ½ cup cherry brandy

3½ oz/100 g/¾ cup all-purpose flour

1¾ oz/50 g/½ cup unsweetened cocoa

½ tsp baking powder

4 eggs

32 fl oz/1 liter/4 cups heavy cream

grated semisweet chocolate

whole fresh cherries, to decorate

method

1 Grease and line a 9-inch/23-cm springform cake pan. Put the halved cherries into a pan, and add 3 tablespoons of the sugar and the cherry brandy. Simmer for 5 minutes. Strain, reserving the syrup. In another bowl, sift together the flour, cocoa, and baking powder.

2 Put the eggs in a heatproof bowl and beat in 5¾ oz/160 g/generous ¾ cup of the sugar. Place the bowl over a pan of simmering water and beat for 6 minutes until thickened. Remove from the heat, then gradually fold in the flour mixture and melted butter. Spoon into the cake pan. Bake in a preheated oven, 350°F/180°C, for 40 minutes. Remove from the oven and let cool.

3 Turn out the cake and cut in half horizontally. Mix the cream with the remaining sugar. Spread the reserved syrup over the cut sides of the cake. Arrange the cherries over one half, top with a layer of cream, and place the other half on top. Cover with cream, press grated chocolate all over, and decorate with cherries.

small
bites

frosted peanut butter cupcakes

ingredients

serves 16

4 tbsp butter, softened,
    or soft margarine
8 oz/225 g/scant 1¼ cups firmly
    packed brown sugar
4 oz/115 g/generous ½ cup
    crunchy peanut butter
2 eggs, lightly beaten
1 tsp vanilla extract
8 oz/225 g/generous
    1½ cups all-purpose flour
2 tsp baking powder
3½ fl oz/100 ml/generous
    ⅓ cup milk

frosting

7 oz/200 g/scant 1 cup
    full-fat soft cream cheese
2 tbsp butter, softened
8 oz/225 g/2 cups confectioners'
    sugar

method

1 Put 16 muffin paper cases in a muffin pan.

2 Put the butter, sugar, and peanut butter in a bowl
and beat together for 1–2 minutes, or until well
mixed. Gradually add the eggs, beating well after each
addition, then add the vanilla extract. Sift in the flour
and baking powder and then, using a metal spoon,
fold them into the mixture, alternating with the milk.
Spoon the batter into the paper cases.

3 Bake the cupcakes in a preheated oven, 350°F/180°C,
for 25 minutes, or until well risen and golden brown.
Transfer to a wire rack and let cool.

4 To make the frosting, put the cream cheese and butter
in a large bowl and, using an electric hand whisk, beat
together until smooth. Sift the confectioners' sugar
into the mixture, then beat together until well mixed.

5 When the cupcakes are cold, spread the frosting on
top of each cupcake, swirling it with a round-bladed
knife. Store the cupcakes in the refrigerator until ready
to serve.

drizzled honey cupcakes

ingredients

serves 12

3 oz/85 g/generous ½ cup
    self-rising flour
¼ tsp ground cinnamon
pinch of ground cloves
pinch of grated nutmeg
6 tbsp butter, softened
3 oz/85 g/scant ½ cup
    superfine sugar
1 tbsp honey
finely grated rind of 1 orange
2 eggs, lightly beaten
1½ oz/40 g/¼ cup walnut pieces,
    minced

topping

½ oz/15 g/⅛ cup walnut pieces,
    minced
¼ tsp ground cinnamon
2 tbsp honey
juice of 1 orange

method

1 Put 12 paper baking cases in a muffin pan, or place
   12 double-layer paper cases on a cookie sheet.

2 Sift the flour, cinnamon, cloves, and nutmeg together
   into a bowl. Put the butter and sugar in a separate
   bowl and beat together until light and fluffy. Beat in
   the honey and orange rind, then gradually add the
   eggs, beating well after each addition. Using a metal
   spoon, fold in the flour mixture. Stir in the walnuts,
   then spoon the batter into the paper cases.

3 Bake the cupcakes in a preheated oven, 375°F/190°C,
   for 20 minutes, or until well risen and golden brown.
   Transfer to a wire rack and let cool.

4 To make the topping, mix together the walnuts and
   cinnamon. Put the honey and orange juice in a pan
   and heat gently, stirring, until combined.

5 When the cupcakes have almost cooled, prick the tops
   all over with a fork or skewer and then drizzle with the
   warm honey mixture. Sprinkle the walnut mixture over
   the top of each cupcake and serve warm or cold.

sticky gingerbread cupcakes

ingredients

serves 16

4 oz/115 g/generous ¾ cup
    all-purpose flour
2 tsp ground ginger
¾ tsp ground cinnamon
1 piece of preserved
    ginger, minced
¼ tsp baking soda
4 tbsp milk
6 tbsp butter, softened,
    or soft margarine
2½ oz/70 g/generous ⅓ cup firmly
    packed brown sugar
2 tbsp molasses
2 eggs, lightly beaten
pieces of preserved ginger,
    to decorate

frosting

6 tbsp butter, softened
6 oz/175 g/1½ cups
    confectioners' sugar
2 tbsp ginger syrup from the
    preserved ginger jar

method

1 Put 16 paper baking cases in a muffin pan, or place
   16 double-layer paper cases on a cookie sheet.

2 Sift the flour, ground ginger, and cinnamon together
   into a bowl. Add the minced ginger and toss in the
   flour mixture until well coated. In a separate bowl,
   dissolve the baking soda in the milk.

3 Put the butter and sugar in a bowl and beat together
   until fluffy. Beat in the molasses, then gradually add the
   eggs, beating well after each addition. Beat in the flour
   mixture, then gradually beat in the milk. Spoon the
   batter into the paper cases.

4 Bake the cupcakes in a preheated oven, 325°F/160°C,
   for 20 minutes, or until well risen and golden brown.
   Transfer to a wire rack and let cool.

5 To make the frosting, put the butter in a bowl and beat
   until fluffy. Sift in the sugar, add the ginger syrup, and
   beat together until smooth and creamy. Slice the
   preserved ginger into thin slivers or chop finely.

6 When the cupcakes are cold, spread the frosting on top
   of each cupcake, then decorate with pieces of ginger.

banana & pecan cupcakes

ingredients

serves 12

8 oz/225 g/generous
   1½ cups all-purpose flour
1¼ tsp baking powder
¼ tsp baking soda
2 ripe bananas
8 tbsp butter, softened,
   or soft margarine
4 oz/115 g/generous ½ cup
   superfine sugar
½ tsp vanilla extract
2 eggs, lightly beaten
4 tbsp sour cream
2 oz/55 g/½ cup pecans,
   coarsely chopped

topping

8 tbsp butter, softened
4 oz/115 g/1 cup confectioners'
   sugar
1 oz/25 g/¼ cup pecans, minced

method

1 Put 12 paper baking cases in a muffin pan, or place 12 double-layer paper cases on a cookie sheet.

2 Sift together the flour, baking powder, and baking soda. Peel the bananas, put them in a bowl, and mash with a fork.

3 Put the butter, sugar, and vanilla in a bowl and beat together until light and fluffy. Gradually add the eggs, beating well after each addition. Stir in the mashed bananas and sour cream. Using a metal spoon, fold in the sifted flour mixture and chopped nuts, then spoon the batter into the paper cases.

4 Bake the cupcakes in a preheated oven, 375°F/190°C, for 20 minutes, or until well risen and golden brown. Transfer to a wire rack and let cool.

5 To make the topping, beat the butter in a bowl until fluffy. Sift in the confectioners' sugar and mix together well. Spread the frosting on top of each cupcake and sprinkle with the minced pecans before serving.

apple & cinnamon muffins

ingredients

serves 6

3 oz/85 g/scant ²/₃ cup all-purpose
    whole-wheat flour
2¹/₂ oz/70 g/¹/₂ cup all-purpose
    white flour
1¹/₂ tsp baking powder
pinch of salt
1 tsp ground cinnamon
1¹/₂ oz/40 g/scant ¹/₄ cup golden
    superfine sugar
2 small eating apples, peeled,
    cored, and finely chopped
4 fl oz/125 ml/¹/₂ cup milk
1 egg, beaten
4 tbsp butter, melted

topping

12 brown sugar lumps,
    coarsely crushed
¹/₂ tsp ground cinnamon

method

1 Place 6 muffin paper liners in a muffin pan.

2 Sift both flours, baking powder, salt, and cinnamon
   together into a large bowl and stir in the sugar and
   chopped apples. Place the milk, egg, and butter in a
   separate bowl and mix. Add the wet ingredients to the
   dry ingredients and gently stir until just combined.

3 Divide the batter evenly among the paper liners. To
   make the topping, mix the crushed sugar lumps and
   cinnamon together and sprinkle over the muffins.
   Bake in a preheated oven, 400°F/200°C, for 20–25
   minutes, or until risen and golden.

4 Remove the muffins from the oven and serve warm
   or place them on a wire rack and let cool.

moist walnut cupcakes

ingredients

serves 12

3 oz/85 g/¾ cup walnuts
4 tbsp butter, softened
3½ oz/100 g/½ cup
    superfine sugar
grated rind of ½ lemon
2½ oz/70 g/½ cup
    self-rising white flour
2 eggs
12 walnut halves, to decorate

frosting

4 tbsp butter, softened
3 oz/85 g/¾ cup confectioners'
    sugar
grated zest of ½ lemon
1 tsp lemon juice

method

1 Put 12 paper baking cases in a muffin pan, or place
   12 double-layer paper cases on a cookie sheet.

2 Put the walnuts in a food processor and, using a
   pulsating action, blend until finely ground, being
   careful not to overgrind, which will turn them to oil.
   Add the butter, cut into small pieces, along with the
   sugar, lemon rind, flour, and eggs, then blend until
   evenly mixed. Spoon the batter into the paper cases.

3 Bake the cupcakes in a preheated oven, 375°F/190°C,
   for 20 minutes, or until well risen and golden brown.
   Transfer to a wire rack and let cool.

4 To make the frosting, put the butter in a bowl and beat
   until fluffy. Sift in the confectioners' sugar, add the
   lemon zest and juice, and mix well together.

5 When the cupcakes are cold, spread the frosting on top
   of each cupcake and top with a walnut to decorate.

rose petal cupcakes

ingredients

serves 12

8 tbsp butter, softened
4 oz/115 g/generous ½ cup
    superfine sugar
2 eggs, lightly beaten
1 tbsp milk
few drops of extract of rose oil
¼ tsp vanilla extract
6 oz/175 g/scant 1¼ cups
    self-rising white flour

frosting

6 tbsp butter, softened
6 oz/175 g/1½ cups
    confectioners' sugar
pink or purple food coloring
    (optional)
silver dragées (cake decoration
    balls), to decorate

candied rose petals

12–24 rose petals
lightly beaten egg white,
    for brushing
superfine sugar, for sprinkling

method

1 To make the candied rose petals, gently rinse the petals and dry well with paper towels. Carefully brush both sides of a rose petal with egg white, then coat well with superfine sugar. Place on a tray and repeat with the remaining petals. Cover the tray with foil and let dry overnight.

2 Put 12 paper baking cases in a muffin pan, or place 12 double-layer paper cases on a cookie sheet.

3 Put the butter and sugar in a bowl and beat together until light and fluffy. Gradually add the eggs, beating well after each addition. Stir in the milk, rose oil extract, and vanilla extract then, using a metal spoon, fold in the flour. Spoon the batter into the paper cases.

4 Bake the cupcakes in a preheated oven, 400°F/200°C, for 12–15 minutes, or until well risen and golden brown. Transfer to a wire rack and let cool.

5 To make the frosting, put the butter in a large bowl and beat until fluffy. Sift in the confectioners' sugar and mix well together. If wished, add a few drops of pink or purple food coloring to complement the rose petals.

6 When the cupcakes are cold, spread the frosting on top of each cake. Top with 1–2 candied rose petals and sprinkle with silver dragées to decorate.

lemon butterfly cakes

ingredients

serves 12

4 oz/115 g/generous ¾ cup
    self-rising flour
½ tsp baking powder
8 tbsp soft margarine
4 oz/115 g/generous ½ cup
    superfine sugar
2 eggs, lightly beaten
finely grated rind of ½ lemon
2 tbsp milk
confectioners' sugar, for dusting

lemon filling

6 tbsp butter, softened
6 oz/175 g/1½ cups confectioners'
    sugar, plus extra for dusting
1 tbsp lemon juice

method

1 Put 12 paper baking cases in a muffin pan, or place
   12 double-layer paper cases on a cookie sheet.

2 Sift the flour and baking powder into a large bowl.
   Add the margarine, sugar, eggs, lemon rind, and milk
   and, using an electric hand whisk, beat together until
   smooth. Spoon the batter into the paper cases.

3 Bake the cupcakes in a preheated oven, 375°F/190°C,
   for 15–20 minutes, or until well risen and golden
   brown. Transfer to a wire rack and let cool.

4 To make the filling, put the butter in a bowl and
   beat until fluffy. Sift in the confectioners' sugar, add
   the lemon juice, and beat together until smooth
   and creamy.

5 When the cupcakes are cold, use a serrated knife to
   cut a circle from the top of each cupcake and then
   cut each circle in half. Spread or pipe a little of the
   buttercream filling into the center of each cupcake,
   then press the 2 semicircular halves into it at an
   angle, to resemble butterfly wings. Dust with sifted
   confectioners' sugar before serving.

caramel apple cupcakes

ingredients

serves 12

2 apples
1 tbsp lemon juice
9 oz/250 g/2¼ cups all-purpose
    flour
2 tsp baking powder
1½ tsp ground cinnamon
2½ oz/70 g/generous ¼ cup
    light brown sugar
4 tbsp butter, plus extra
    for greasing
3½ fl oz/100 ml/scant ½ cup milk
3½ fl oz/100 ml/scant ½ cup
    apple juice
1 egg, beaten

caramel topping

2 tbsp light cream
1½ oz/40 g/3 tbsp light brown
    sugar
½ oz/15 g/ tbsp butter

method

1 Grease a 12-cup muffin pan (preferably nonstick).

2 Core and coarsely grate one of the apples. Slice the
    remaining apple into ¼ inch/5 mm thick wedges and
    toss in the lemon juice. Sift together the flour, baking
    powder, and cinnamon, then stir in the sugar and
    grated apple.

3 Melt the butter and mix with the milk, apple juice, and
    egg. Stir the liquid mixture into the dry ingredients,
    mixing lightly until just combined.

4 Spoon the batter into the prepared muffin pan.
    Put two apple slices on top of each cake.

5 Bake in a preheated oven, 400°F/200°C, for 20–25
    minutes, or until risen, firm, and golden brown. Run
    a knife around the edge of each cake to loosen, then
    turn out onto a wire rack to cool.

6 For the caramel topping, place all the ingredients in
    a small saucepan and heat, stirring, until the sugar
    has dissolved. Increase the heat and boil rapidly for
    2 minutes, or until slightly thickened and syrupy.
    Cool slightly, then drizzle over the cakes and let set.

warm molten-centered chocolate cupcakes

ingredients

serves 8

4 tbsp soft margarine
2 oz/55 g/generous ¼ cup
    superfine sugar
1 large egg
3 oz/85 g/generous ½ cup
    self-rising flour
1 tbsp unsweetened cocoa
2 oz/55 g semisweet chocolate
confectioners' sugar, for dusting

method

1 Put 8 paper baking cases in a muffin pan, or place 8 double-layer paper cases on a cookie sheet.

2 Put the margarine, sugar, egg, flour, and cocoa in a large bowl and, using an electric hand whisk, beat together until just smooth.

3 Spoon half of the batter into the paper cases. Using a teaspoon, make an indentation in the center of each cake. Break the chocolate evenly into 8 squares and place a piece in each indentation, then spoon the remaining cake batter on top.

4 Bake the cupcakes in a preheated oven, 375°F/190°C, for 20 minutes, or until well risen and springy to the touch. Leave the cupcakes for 2–3 minutes before serving warm, dusted with sifted confectioners' sugar.

low-fat blueberry muffins

ingredients

serves 12

8 oz/225 g/generous 1½ cups
    all-purpose flour
1 tsp baking soda
¼ tsp salt
1 tsp allspice
4 oz/115 g/generous ½ cup
    superfine sugar
3 egg whites
3 tbsp lowfat margarine
5 fl oz/50 ml/⅔ cup thick lowfat
    plain yogurt or blueberry-
    flavored yogurt
1 tsp vanilla extract
3 oz/85 g/¾ cup fresh blueberries

method

1 Place 12 muffin paper liners in a muffin pan.

2 Sift the flour, baking soda, salt, and half of the allspice into a large mixing bowl. Add 6 tablespoons of the superfine sugar and mix together.

3 In a separate bowl, whisk the egg whites together. Add the margarine, yogurt, and vanilla extract and mix together well, then stir in the blueberries until thoroughly mixed. Add to the flour mixture, then gently stir together until just combined. Do not overstir the batter—it is fine for it to be a little lumpy.

4 Divide the muffin batter evenly among the paper liners (they should be about two-thirds full). Mix the remaining sugar with the remaining allspice, then sprinkle the mixture over the muffins.

5 Bake in a preheated oven, 375°F/190°C, for 25 minutes or until risen and golden. Remove the muffins from the oven and serve warm, or place them on a wire rack and let cool.

white chocolate brownies

ingredients

serves 9

4 oz/115 g unsalted butter,
    plus extra for greasing
8 oz/225 g white chocolate
4 oz/115 g/¾ cup walnut pieces
2 eggs
4 oz/115 g/generous ½ cup soft
    brown sugar
4 oz/115 g/generous ⅔ cup
    self-rising flour

method

1 Lightly grease a 7-inch/18-cm square cake pan
   with butter.

2 Coarsely chop 6 oz/175 g of chocolate and all the
   walnuts. Put the remaining chocolate and the butter
   in a heatproof bowl set over a pan of gently simmering
   water. When melted, stir together, then set aside to
   cool slightly.

3 Whisk the eggs and sugar together, then beat in the
   cooled chocolate mixture until well mixed. Fold in the
   flour, chopped chocolate, and the walnuts. Turn the
   mixture into the prepared pan and smooth the surface.

4 Transfer the pan to a preheated oven, 350°F/180°C,
   and bake for 30 minutes, or until just set. The mixture
   should still be a little soft in the center. Remove from
   the oven and let cool in the pan, then cut into
   9 squares before serving.

devil's food cakes with chocolate icing

ingredients

serves 18

3½ tbsp soft margarine
4 oz/115 g/generous ½ cup firmly
    packed brown sugar
2 large eggs
4 oz/115 g/generous ¾ cup
    all-purpose flour
½ tsp baking soda
1 oz/25 g/generous ¼ cup
    unsweetened cocoa
4 fl oz/125 ml/½ cup sour cream

frosting

4½ oz/125 g semisweet chocolate
2 tbsp superfine sugar
5 fl oz/150 ml/⅔ cup sour cream

chocolate curls (optional)

3½ oz/100 g semisweet chocolate

method

1 Put 18 paper baking cases in a muffin pan, or put 18 double-layer paper cases on a cookie sheet.

2 Put the margarine, sugar, eggs, flour, baking soda, and cocoa in a large bowl and, using an electric hand whisk, beat together until just smooth. Using a metal spoon, fold in the sour cream. Spoon the batter into the paper cases.

3 Bake the cupcakes in a preheated oven, 350°F/180°C, for 20 minutes, or until well risen and firm to the touch. Transfer to a wire rack to cool.

4 To make the frosting, break the chocolate into a heatproof bowl. Set the bowl over a pan of gently simmering water and heat until melted, stirring occasionally.

5 Remove from the heat and let cool slightly, then whisk in the sugar and sour cream until combined. Spread the frosting over the tops of the cupcakes and let set in the refrigerator before serving. If liked, serve decorated with chocolate curls made by shaving semisweet chocolate with a potato peeler.

fig & almond muffins

ingredients

serves 12

2 tbsp sunflower or peanut oil,
  plus extra for oiling (if using)
9 oz/250 g/generous 1¾ cups
  all-purpose flour
1 tsp baking soda
½ tsp salt
8 oz/225 g/1 cup raw sugar
3 oz/85 g/generous ½ cup dried
  figs, chopped
4 oz/115 g/1 cup almonds,
  chopped
8 fl oz/250 ml/1 cup water
1 tsp almond extract
2 tbsp chopped almonds,
  to decorate

method

1 Oil a 12-cup muffin pan with sunflower oil, or line it with 12 muffin paper liners. Sift the flour, baking soda, and salt into a mixing bowl. Then add the raw sugar and stir together.

2 In a separate bowl, mix the figs, almonds, and remaining sunflower oil together. Then stir in the water and almond extract. Add the fruit and nut mixture to the flour mixture and gently stir together. Do not overstir—it is fine for it to be a little lumpy.

3 Divide the muffin batter evenly among the 12 cups in the muffin pan or the paper liners (they should be about two-thirds full), then sprinkle over the remaining chopped almonds to decorate. Transfer to a preheated oven, 375°F/190°C, and bake for 25 minutes, or until risen and golden.

4 Remove the muffins from the oven and serve warm, or place them on a wire rack and let cool.

fudge nut muffins

ingredients

serves 12

9 oz/250 g/generous 1¾ cups
    all-purpose flour
4 tsp baking powder
3 oz/85 g/scant ½ cup
    superfine sugar
6 tbsp crunchy peanut butter
1 large egg, beaten
4 tbsp butter, melted
6 fl oz/175 ml/¾ cup milk
5½ oz/150 g vanilla fudge,
    cut into small pieces
3 tbsp coarsely chopped
    unsalted peanuts

method

1 Line a 12-cup muffin pan with double muffin paper liners. Sift the flour and baking powder into a bowl. Stir in the superfine sugar. Add the peanut butter and stir until the mixture resembles bread crumbs.

2 Place the egg, butter, and milk in a separate bowl and beat until blended, then stir into the dry ingredients until just blended. Lightly stir in the fudge pieces. Divide the batter evenly among the muffin liners.

3 Sprinkle the chopped peanuts on top and bake in a preheated oven, 400°F/200°C, for 20–25 minutes until well risen and firm to the touch. Remove the muffins from the oven and let cool for 2 minutes, then place them on a wire rack and let cool completely.

variation

For a special treat, try a flavored fudge, such as caramel, mint, banana, or even a whiskey-flavored fudge!

spiced chocolate muffins

ingredients

serves 12

3½ oz/100 g butter, softened

5 oz/150 g/scant ¾ cup
   superfine sugar

4 oz/115 g/½ cup packed
   brown sugar

2 large eggs

5 fl oz/150 ml/⅔ cup sour cream

5 tbsp milk

9 oz/250 g/generous
   1¾ cups all-purpose flour

1 tsp baking soda

2 tbsp unsweetened cocoa

1 tsp allspice

7 oz/200 g/generous 1 cup
   semisweet chocolate chips

method

1 Line a 12-cup muffin pan with muffin liners.

2 Place the butter, superfine sugar, and brown sugar in
   a bowl and beat well. Beat in the eggs, sour cream, and
   milk until thoroughly mixed. Sift the flour, baking soda,
   cocoa, and allspice into a separate bowl and stir into
   the mixture. Add the chocolate chips and mix well.
   Divide the batter evenly among the paper liners. Bake
   in a preheated oven, 375°F/190°C, for 25–30 minutes.

3 Remove the muffins from the oven and let cool for
   10 minutes. Place them on a wire rack and let cool
   completely. Store in an airtight container until required.

fruit & nut squares

ingredients

serves 9

4 oz/115 g unsalted butter,
  plus extra for greasing
2 tbsp honey
1 egg, beaten
3 oz/85 g/generous ¾ cup
  ground almonds
4 oz/115 g/scant 1 cup
  no-soak dried apricots, finely
  chopped
2 oz/55 g/⅓ cup dried cherries
2 oz/55 g/generous ¼ cup toasted
  chopped hazelnuts
1 oz/25 g/⅛ cup sesame seeds
3 oz/85 g/scant 1 cup rolled oats

method

1 Lightly grease a 7-inch/18-cm shallow, square baking pan with butter. Beat the remaining butter with the honey in a bowl until creamy, then beat in the egg with the almonds.

2 Add the remaining ingredients and mix together. Press into the prepared pan, ensuring that the mixture is firmly packed. Smooth the top.

3 Bake in a preheated oven, 350°F/180°C, for 20–25 minutes, or until firm to the touch and golden brown.

4 Remove from the oven and let stand for 10 minutes before marking into squares. Let stand until cold before removing from the pan. Store in an airtight container.

strawberry petits choux

ingredients

serves 12

filling and topping

2 tsp powdered gelatin
2 tbsp water
12 oz/350 g/3 cups strawberries,
    hulled, ⅓ sliced
8 oz/225 g/1 cup ricotta cheese
1 tbsp superfine sugar
2 tsp strawberry-flavored liqueur
confectioners' sugar, for dusting

petits choux

3½ oz/100 g/¾ cup all-purpose flour
2 tbsp unsweetened cocoa
pinch of salt
6 tbsp butter
1 cup water
2 eggs, plus 1 egg white, beaten

method

1 Sprinkle the gelatin over the water in a heatproof bowl to soften. Place the bowl over a saucepan of gently simmering water and stir until the gelatin dissolves.

2 Place a scant 1 cup of the strawberries in a blender with the ricotta cheese, sugar, and liqueur. Add the gelatin and process briefly. Transfer to a bowl, cover and chill for 1–1½ hours, until set. Line a cookie sheet with parchment paper.

3 To make the petits choux, sift together the flour, cocoa and salt. Put the butter and water into a heavy-bottom saucepan and heat gently until the butter has melted. Remove the pan from the heat and add the flour, cocoa, and salt all at once, stirring well. Let cool slightly.

4 Gradually beat the eggs and egg white into the flour paste until it is smooth and glossy. Drop 12 rounded tablespoonfuls of the mixture onto the prepared cookie sheet and bake in a preheated oven, 425°F/ 220°C, for 20–25 minutes, until puffed up and crisp. Make a slit in the side of each petit chou. Return to the oven for 5 minutes, then transfer to a wire rack.

5 Cut the petits choux in half, divide the mousse and strawberry slices among them, then replace the tops. Dust lightly with confectioners' sugar and place in the refrigerator. Serve within 1½ hours.

chocolate chip cookies

ingredients

serves 30

6 oz/175 g/1½ cups all-purpose flour
1 tsp baking powder
4½ oz/125 g soft margarine, plus extra for greasing
3 oz/85 g/½ cup light brown sugar
2 oz/55 g/¼ cup superfine sugar
½ tsp vanilla extract
1 egg
4½ oz/125 g/⅔ cup semisweet chocolate chips

method

1 Lightly grease two cookie sheets.

2 Place all of the ingredients in a large mixing bowl and beat until thoroughly combined.

3 Place tablespoonfuls of the mixture onto the cookie sheets, spacing them well apart to allow for spreading during cooking.

4 Bake in a preheated oven, 375°F/190°C, for 10–12 minutes, or until the cookies are golden brown.

5 Using a spatula, transfer the cookies to a wire rack to cool completely.

shortbread

ingredients

serves 8

6 oz/175 g/scant 1½ cups
    all-purpose flour, plus extra
    for dusting
pinch of salt
2 oz/55 g/¼ cup superfine sugar,
    plus extra for sprinkling
4 oz/115 g butter, cut into small
    pieces, plus extra for greasing

method

1 Grease an 8-inch/20-cm fluted round tart pan.

2 Mix together the flour, salt, and sugar. Rub the butter into the dry ingredients. Continue to work the mixture until it forms a soft dough. Make sure you do not overwork the shortbread or it will be tough, not crumbly as it should be.

3 Lightly press the dough into the prepared tart pan. If you don't have a fluted pan, roll out the dough on a lightly floured board, place on a cookie sheet, and pinch the edges to form a scalloped pattern.

4 Mark into eight pieces with a knife. Prick all over with a fork and bake in the center of a preheated oven, 300°F/150°C, for 45–50 minutes, until the shortbread is firm and just colored.

5 Let cool in the pan and sprinkle with the sugar. Cut into portions and transfer to a wire rack.

variation

For an extra-indulgent version, add 1½ oz/40 g of chocolate chips to the shortbread surface just after pressing the dough into the prepared tart pan (step 3).

lavender biscuits

ingredients

serves 12

2 oz/55 g/¼ cup golden
    superfine sugar, plus
    extra for dusting
1 tsp chopped lavender leaves
4 oz/115 g butter, softened,
    plus extra for greasing
finely grated rind of 1 lemon
6 oz/175 g/1¼ cups all-purpose
    flour

method

1 Place the sugar and lavender leaves in a food processor. Process until the lavender is very finely chopped, then add the butter and lemon rind and process until light and fluffy. Transfer to a large bowl. Sift in the flour and beat until the mixture forms a stiff dough.

2 Place the dough on a sheet of parchment paper and place another sheet on top. Gently press down with a rolling pin and roll out to ⅛–¼-inch/3–5-mm thick. Remove the top sheet of paper and stamp out circles from the dough using a 2¾-inch/7-cm round cookie cutter. Re-knead and re-roll the dough trimmings and stamp out more cookies.

3 Using a spatula, carefully transfer the cookies to a large, greased cookie sheet. Prick the cookies with a fork and bake in a preheated oven, 300°F/150°C, for 12 minutes, or until pale golden brown. Let cool on the cookie sheet for 2 minutes, then transfer to a wire rack to cool completely, and dust with superfine sugar.

desserts

apple pie

ingredients

serves 6–8

pie dough

6 oz/175 g/2 cups all-purpose
flour

pinch of salt

3 oz/85 g butter or margarine,
cut into small pieces

3 oz/85 g lard or vegetable
shortening, cut into
small pieces

about 6 tbsp cold water

beaten egg or milk, for glazing

filling

1 lb 10 oz–2 lb 4 oz/750 g–1 kg
baking apples, peeled, cored,
and sliced

4½ oz/125 g/scant ⅔ cup light
brown sugar or superfine
sugar, plus extra for sprinkling

½–1 tsp ground cinnamon,
allspice, or ground ginger

about 1–2 tbsp water (optional)

method

1 To make the pie dough, sift the flour and salt into a
large bowl. Add the butter and lard and rub in until the
mixture resembles fine breadcrumbs. Add the water
to make a dough. Wrap the dough and let chill in the
refrigerator for 30 minutes.

2 Roll out almost two thirds of the pie dough thinly and
use to line a deep 9-inch/23-cm pie plate.

3 For the filling, mix the apples with the sugar and spice
and pack into the pastry shell; the filling can come up
above the rim. Add the water if needed, particularly if
the apples are not very juicy. Roll out the remaining pie
dough to form a lid. Dampen the edges of the pie rim
with water and position the lid, pressing the edges
firmly together. Trim and crimp the edges.

4 Use the pastry trimmings to cut out leaves or other
shapes to decorate the top of the pie. Glaze the top of
the pie with beaten egg or milk, make one or two slits
in the top, and place the pie on a baking sheet.

5 Bake in a preheated oven, 425°F/220°C for 20 minutes,
then reduce the temperature to 350°F/180°C and
bake for an additional 30 minutes, or until the pastry
is a light golden brown. Serve hot or cold, sprinkled
with sugar.

latticed cherry pie

ingredients

serves 8

pie dough

5 oz/140 g/1 cup all-purpose flour,
    plus extra for dusting
¼ tsp baking powder
½ tsp allspice
½ tsp salt
1¾ oz/50 g/¼ cup superfine sugar
2 oz/55 g cold unsalted butter,
    diced, plus extra for greasing
1 egg, beaten, plus extra
    for glazing

filling

2 lb/900 g pitted fresh cherries
    or canned cherries, drained
5 oz/150 g/½ cup superfine sugar
½ tsp almond extract
2 tsp cherry brandy
¼ tsp allspice
2 tbsp cornstarch
2 tbsp water
2 tbsp unsalted butter, diced

method

1 To make the pie dough, sift the flour and baking
powder into a large bowl. Stir in the allspice, salt, and
sugar. Rub in the butter until the mixture resembles fine
breadcrumbs. Add the beaten egg and mix to a firm
dough. Cut the dough in half and roll each half into a
ball. Wrap and chill in the refrigerator for 30 minutes.

2 Grease a 9-inch/23-cm round tart pan. Roll out the pie
dough into two 12-inch/30-cm rounds. Use one to line
the tart pan, trimming the edge to leave an overhang of
½ inch/1 cm.

3 To make the filling, simmer half the cherries with the
sugar over a low heat, until the sugar has dissolved. Stir
in the almond extract, brandy, and allspice. Mix the
cornstarch and water to form a paste. Stir in the paste,
then return to the heat and stir continuously until
the mixture boils and thickens. Stir in the remaining
cherries, pour into the pastry shell, and dot with butter.

4 Cut the remaining dough round into long strips about
½ inch/1 cm wide and form a lattice over the cherries.
Trim off the ends and seal the edges with water. Crimp
around the rim, then brush the top with beaten egg to
glaze. Cover with foil, then bake in a preheated oven,
425°F/220°C for 30 minutes. Discard the foil, then bake
for an additional 15 minutes, or until golden.

forest fruit pie

ingredients

serves 4–6

filling

8 oz/225 g/1⅛ cups blueberries
8 oz/225 g/1⅛ cups raspberries
8 oz/225 g/1⅛ cups blackberries
3½ oz/100 g/½ cup superfine sugar
2 tbsp confectioners' sugar,
    to decorate
whipped cream, to serve

pie dough

8 oz/225 g/1¼ cups all-purpose
    flour, plus extra for dusting
1 oz/25 g/generous ¼ cup
    ground hazelnuts
3½ oz/100 g butter, cut into small
    pieces, plus extra for greasing
finely grated rind of 1 lemon
1 egg yolk, beaten
4 tbsp milk

method

1 Place the fruit in a pan with 3 tablespoons of the superfine sugar and let simmer gently, stirring frequently, for 5 minutes. Remove the pan from the heat.

2 Sift the flour into a bowl, then add the hazelnuts. Rub in the butter with the fingertips until the mixture resembles bread crumbs, then sift in the remaining sugar. Add the lemon rind, egg yolk, and 3 tablespoons of the milk and mix. Turn out on to a lightly floured counter and knead briefly. Wrap and let chill in the refrigerator for 30 minutes.

3 Grease an 8-inch/20-cm pie dish with butter. Roll out two-thirds of the pie dough to a thickness of ¼ inch/ 5 mm and use it to line the base and side of the dish. Spoon the fruit into the pastry shell. Brush the rim with water, then roll out the remaining pie dough to cover the pie. Trim and crimp round the edge, then make 2 small slits in the top and decorate with 2 leaf shapes cut out from the dough trimmings. Brush all over with the remaining milk. Bake in a preheated oven, 375°F/ 190°C, for 40 minutes.

4 Remove the pie from the oven, sprinkle with the confectioners' sugar and serve with whipped cream.

mississippi mud pie

ingredients

serves 8

pie dough

8 oz/225 g/1¼ cups all-purpose
    flour, plus extra for dusting
2 tbsp unsweetened cocoa
5½ oz/150 g butter
2 tbsp superfine sugar
1–2 tbsp cold water

filling

6 oz/175 g butter
12 oz/350 g/scant 1¾ cups
    packed brown sugar
4 eggs, lightly beaten
4 tbsp unsweetened cocoa, sifted
5½ oz/150 g semisweet chocolate
10 fl oz/300 ml/1¼ cups
    light cream
1 tsp chocolate extract

to decorate

15 fl oz/425 ml/scant 2 cups
    heavy cream, whipped
chocolate flakes and curls

method

1 To make the pie dough, sift the flour and cocoa into a
   mixing bowl. Rub in the butter with the fingertips until
   the mixture resembles fine bread crumbs. Stir in the
   sugar and enough cold water to mix to a soft dough.
   Wrap the dough and let chill in the refrigerator for
   15 minutes.

2 Roll out the dough on a lightly floured counter and
   use to line a 9-inch/23-cm loose-bottom tart pan or
   ceramic pie dish. Line with parchment paper and fill
   with dried beans. Bake in a preheated oven, 375°F/
   190°C, for 15 minutes. Remove from the oven and take
   out the paper and beans. Bake the tart shell for an
   additional 10 minutes.

3 To make the filling, beat the butter and sugar together
   in a bowl and gradually beat in the eggs with the
   cocoa. Melt the chocolate and beat it into the mixture
   with the light cream and the chocolate extract.

4 Reduce the oven temperature to 325°F/160°C. Pour
   the mixture into the tart shell and bake for 45 minutes,
   or until the filling has set gently.

5 Let the mud pie cool completely, then transfer it to
   a serving plate, if you like. Cover with the whipped
   cream. Decorate the pie with chocolate flakes and
   curls and then let chill until ready to serve.

banana toffee pie

ingredients

serves 8

filling

3 x 14 oz/400 g cans
  sweetened condensed milk
4 ripe bananas
juice of ½ lemon
1 tsp vanilla extract
2¾ oz/75 g semisweet
  chocolate, grated
16 fl oz/475 ml/2 cups heavy
  cream, whipped

cookie crust

3 oz/85 g butter, melted,
  plus extra for greasing
5½ oz/150 g graham crackers,
  crushed into crumbs
1 oz/25 g/scant ⅓ cup
  shelled almonds,
  toasted and ground
1 oz/25 g/scant ⅓ cup
  shelled hazelnuts,
  toasted and ground

method

1 Place the unopened cans of milk in a large pan and add enough water to cover them. Bring to a boil, then reduce the heat and let simmer for 2 hours, topping up the water level to keep the cans covered. Carefully lift out the hot cans from the pan and let cool.

2 Place the butter in a bowl and add the crushed graham crackers and ground nuts. Mix together well, then press the mixture evenly into the base and side of a greased 9-inch/23-cm tart pan. Bake in a preheated oven, 350°F/180°C, for 10–12 minutes, then remove from the oven and let cool.

3 Peel and slice the bananas and place in a bowl. Squeeze over the juice from the lemon, add the vanilla extract, and mix together. Spread the banana mixture over the cookie crust in the pan, then spoon over the contents of the cooled cans of condensed milk.

4 Sprinkle over 1¾ oz/50 g of the chocolate, then top with a layer of whipped cream. Sprinkle over the remaining grated chocolate and serve the pie at room temperature.

pecan pie

ingredients

serves 8

pie dough

9 oz/250 g/scant 1⅝ cups
all-purpose flour
pinch of salt
4 oz/115 g butter, cut into
small pieces
1 tbsp lard or vegetable
shortening, cut into
small pieces
2 oz/55 g/generous ¼ cup golden
superfine sugar
6 tbsp cold milk

filling

3 eggs
8 oz/250 g/generous 1 cup
dark brown sugar
1 tsp vanilla extract
pinch of salt
3 oz/85 g butter, melted
3 tbsp corn syrup
3 tbsp molasses
12 oz/350 g/2 cups shelled
pecans, roughly chopped
pecan halves, to decorate
whipped cream or vanilla ice
cream, to serve

method

1 To make the pie dough, sift the flour and salt into
a mixing bowl and rub in the butter and lard with
the fingertips until the mixture resembles fine bread
crumbs. Work in the superfine sugar and add the milk.
Work the mixture into a soft dough. Wrap the dough
and let chill in the refrigerator for 30 minutes.

2 Roll out the pie dough and use it to line a 9–10-inch/
23–25-cm tart pan. Trim off the excess by running the
rolling pin over the top of the tart pan. Line with
parchment paper, and fill with dried beans. Bake in a
preheated oven, 400°F/200°C, for 20 minutes. Take out
of the oven and remove the paper and dried beans.
Reduce the oven temperature to 350°F/180°C. Place
a baking sheet in the oven.

3 To make the filling, place the eggs in a bowl and beat
lightly. Beat in the dark brown sugar, vanilla extract, and
salt. Stir in the butter, syrup, molasses, and chopped
nuts. Pour into the pastry shell and decorate with the
pecan halves.

4 Place on the heated baking sheet and bake in the oven
for 35-40 minutes until the filling is set. Serve warm or
at room temperature with whipped cream or vanilla
ice cream.

lemon meringue pie

ingredients

serves 8–10

butter, for greasing
all-purpose flour, for dusting
9 oz/250 g ready-made pie dough,
    thawed if frozen
3 tbsp cornstarch
3 oz/85 g/scant ½ cup
    superfine sugar
grated rind of 3 lemons
10 fl oz/300 ml/1¼ cups
    cold water
5 fl oz/150 ml/⅔ cup
    lemon juice
3 egg yolks
2 oz/55 g unsalted butter,
    cut into small cubes

meringue

3 egg whites
6 oz/175 g/¾ cup superfine sugar
1 tsp golden granulated sugar

method

1 Grease a 10-inch/25-cm fluted tart pan. On a lightly floured counter, roll out the pie dough and ease it into the pan. Prick the bottom of the tart shell and let chill, uncovered, for 20–30 minutes. Line the shell with parchment paper and fill with dried beans. Bake on a preheated cookie sheet in a preheated oven, 400°F/200°C, for 15 minutes. Remove the beans and paper and return to the oven for 10 minutes. Remove and reduce the temperature to 300°F/150°C.

2 Put the cornstarch, sugar, and lemon rind into a pan. Blend in a little of the water to make a smooth paste. Add the remaining water and the lemon juice. Bring to a boil over medium heat, stirring continuously. Let simmer gently for 1 minute until smooth and glossy. Remove from the heat. Beat in the egg yolks, 1 at a time, then the butter. Place the pan in a bowl of cold water to cool the filling, then spoon it into the tart shell.

3 To make the meringue, whisk the egg whites until soft peaks form. Gradually add the superfine sugar, whisking well. Spoon the meringue over the filling to cover it completely. Swirl the meringue into peaks and sprinkle with granulated sugar. Bake for 20–30 minutes until the meringue is crispy and pale gold (the center should still be soft). Let cool slightly before serving.

baked lemon cheesecake

ingredients

serves 6–8

2 oz/55 g butter, plus extra for greasing
6 oz/175 g crushed gingersnaps
3 lemons
10½ oz/300 g/1⅓ cups ricotta cheese
7 oz/200 g/scant 1 cup Greek-style yogurt or strained plain yogurt
4 eggs
1 tbsp cornstarch
½ cup superfine sugar
strips of lemon rind, to decorate
confectioners' sugar, for dusting

method

1 Lightly grease an 8-inch/20-cm round springform pan and line the bottom with nonstick parchment paper.

2 Melt the butter and stir in the cookie crumbs. Press into the bottom of the prepared cake pan. Chill until firm.

3 Meanwhile, finely grate the rind and squeeze the juice from the lemons. Add the ricotta, yogurt, eggs, cornstarch, and superfine sugar and whip until a smooth batter is formed.

4 Carefully pour the batter into the pan. Bake in a preheated oven, 350°F/180°C for 40–45 minutes, or until just firm and golden brown.

5 Cool the cheesecake completely in the pan, then run a knife around the edge to loosen and turn out onto a serving plate. Decorate with lemon rind and dust with confectioners' sugar.

new york cheesecake

ingredients

serves 8–10

6 tbsp butter

7 oz/200 g graham crackers, crushed

sunflower oil, for brushing

14 oz/400 g/1¾ cups cream cheese

2 large eggs

5 oz/140 g/¾ cup superfine sugar

1½ tsp vanilla extract

16 fl oz/450 ml/2 cups sour cream

blueberry topping

2 oz/55 g/generous ¼ cup superfine sugar

4 tbsp water

9 oz/250 g/generous 1½ cups fresh blueberries

1 tsp arrowroot

method

1 Melt the butter in a pan over low heat. Stir in the crackers, then spread in an 8-inch/20-cm springform pan brushed with oil. Place the cream cheese, eggs, ½ cup of the sugar, and ½ teaspoon of the vanilla extract in a food processor. Process until smooth. Pour over the cracker base and smooth the top. Place on a cookie sheet and bake in a preheated oven, 375°F/ 190°C, for 20 minutes until set. Remove from the oven and leave for 20 minutes. Leave the oven switched on.

2 Mix the cream with the remaining sugar and vanilla extract in a bowl. Spoon over the cheesecake. Return it to the oven for 10 minutes, let cool, then chill in the refrigerator for 8 hours, or overnight.

3 To make the topping, place the sugar in a pan with 2 tablespoons of the water over low heat and stir until the sugar has dissolved. Increase the heat, add the blueberries, cover, and cook for a few minutes, or until they begin to soften. Remove from the heat. Mix the arrowroot and remaining water in a bowl, add to the fruit, and stir until smooth. Return to low heat. Cook until the juice thickens and turns translucent. Let cool.

4 Remove the cheesecake from the pan 1 hour before serving. Spoon the fruit topping over and let chill until ready to serve.

raspberry vacherin

ingredients

serves 10

3 egg whites
6 oz/175 g/³⁄₄ cup superfine sugar
1 tsp cornstarch
1 oz/25 g semisweet chocolate,
    grated

filling and topping

6 oz/175 g semisweet chocolate,
    broken into pieces
16 fl oz/450 ml/2 cups heavy
    cream, whipped
10 oz/280 g/2 cups fresh
    raspberries
a little melted chocolate,
    to decorate

method

1 Draw three rectangles, measuring 4 x 10 inches/
  10 x 25 cm, on sheets of parchment paper and place
  on two cookie sheets.

2 Whisk the egg whites in a mixing bowl until soft
  peaks form, then gradually whisk in half of the sugar
  and continue whisking until the mixture is very stiff
  and glossy. Carefully fold in the remaining sugar, the
  cornstarch, and the grated chocolate.

3 Spoon the meringue mixture into a pastry bag fitted
  with a ¹⁄₂-inch/1-cm plain tip and pipe lines across the
  rectangles. Bake in a preheated oven, 275°F/140°C, for
  1¹⁄₂ hours, changing the position of the cookie sheets
  halfway through. Then turn off the oven and leave the
  meringues to cool inside the oven.

4 Place the chocolate in a heatproof bowl set over a
  saucepan of simmering water until melted. Spread the
  chocolate over two of the meringue layers. Let set.
  Place one chocolate-coated meringue on a plate and
  top with about one third of the cream and raspberries.
  Gently place the second chocolate-coated meringue
  on top and spread with half of the remaining cream
  and raspberries. Place the last meringue on the
  top and decorate with the remaining cream and
  raspberries. Drizzle over melted chocolate and serve.

strawberry roulade

ingredients

serves 8

3 eggs

4¹/₂ oz/125 g/²/₃ cup superfine sugar

4¹/₂ oz/125 g/scant 1 cup
all-purpose flour

1 tbsp hot water

1 tbsp toasted slivered almonds,
to decorate

filling

7 fl oz/200 ml/³/₄ cup low-fat
Mascarpone cheese

1 tsp almond extract

1¹/₂ cups small strawberries

method

1 Line a 14 x 10-inch/35 x 25-cm jelly roll pan with
parchment paper.

2 Place the eggs in a heatproof bowl with the superfine
sugar. Place the bowl over a saucepan of hot water and
whisk until pale and thick.

3 Remove the bowl from the pan. Sift in the flour and
fold into the egg mixture along with the hot water.
Pour the batter into the prepared pan and bake in a
preheated oven, 425°F/220°C for 8–10 minutes, until
golden and springy to the touch.

4 Turn out the cake onto a sheet of parchment paper.
Peel off the lining paper and roll up the cake tightly
along with the parchment paper. Wrap in a clean dish
towel and let cool.

5 For the filling, mix together the Mascarpone cheese
and the almond extract. Wash, hull, and slice the
strawberries. Chill the Mascarpone mixture and the
strawberries in the refrigerator until ready to use.

6 Unroll the cake, spread the Mascarpone mixture over
the surface, and sprinkle with sliced strawberries. Roll
up the cake again (without the parchment paper this
time) and transfer to a serving plate. Sprinkle with
slivered almonds and serve.

pear & pecan strudel

ingredients

serves 4–6

2 ripe pears
4 tbsp butter
2 oz/55 g/1 cup fresh white
    bread crumbs
2 oz/55 g/generous ⅓ cup shelled
    pecans, chopped
1 oz/25 g/scant ¼ cup
    dark brown sugar
finely grated rind of 1 orange
3½ oz/100 g filo pastry, thawed
    if frozen
6 tbsp orange blossom honey
2 tbsp orange juice
sifted confectioners' sugar,
    for dusting
strained plain yogurt, to serve
    (optional)

method

1 Peel, core, and chop the pears. Melt 1 tablespoon of the butter in a skillet and gently sauté the bread crumbs until golden. Transfer the bread crumbs to a bowl and add the pears, nuts, dark brown sugar, and orange rind. Place the remaining butter in a small pan and heat until melted.

2 Set aside 1 sheet of filo pastry, keeping it well wrapped and brush the remaining filo sheets with a little melted butter. Spoon a little of the nut filling onto 1 buttered filo sheet, leaving a 1-inch/2.5-cm margin around the edge. Build up the strudel by placing the remaining buttered filo sheets on top of the first, spreading each one with nut filling as you build up the layers. Drizzle the honey and orange juice over the top.

3 Fold the short ends over the filling, then roll up, starting at a long side. Carefully lift onto a baking sheet with the join uppermost. Brush with any remaining melted butter and crumple the reserved sheet of filo pastry around the strudel. Bake in a preheated oven, 400°F/200°C, for 25 minutes, or until golden and crisp. Dust with sifted confectioners' sugar and serve warm with strained plain yogurt, if using.

peach cobbler

ingredients

serves 4–6

filling

6 peaches, peeled and sliced
4 tbsp superfine sugar
½ tbsp lemon juice
1½ tsp cornstarch
½ tsp almond or vanilla extract
vanilla or pecan ice cream,
    to serve

topping

6 oz/175 g/scant 1¼ cups
    all-purpose flour
4 oz/115 g/generous ½ cup
    superfine sugar
1½ tsp baking powder
½ tsp salt
3 oz/85 g butter, diced
1 egg
5–6 tbsp milk

method

1 Place the peaches in a 9-inch/23-cm square ovenproof dish that is also suitable for serving. Add the sugar, lemon juice, cornstarch, and almond extract and toss together. Bake the peaches in a preheated oven, 425°F/220°C, for 20 minutes.

2 Meanwhile, to make the topping, sift the flour, all but 2 tablespoons of the sugar, the baking powder, and salt into a bowl. Rub in the butter with the fingertips until the mixture resembles bread crumbs. Mix the egg and 5 tablespoons of the milk in a pitcher, then mix into the dry ingredients with a fork until a soft, sticky dough forms. If the dough seems too dry, stir in the extra tablespoon of milk.

3 Reduce the oven temperature to 400°F/200°C. Remove the peaches from the oven and drop spoonfuls of the topping over the surface, without smoothing. Sprinkle with the remaining sugar, return to the oven, and bake for an additional 15 minutes, or until the topping is golden brown and firm—the topping will spread as it cooks. Serve hot or at room temperature with ice cream.

almond tart

ingredients

serves 8

pie dough

10 oz/280 g/2 cups all-purpose
flour, plus extra for dusting
5½ oz/150 g/generous
¾ cup superfine sugar
1 tsp finely grated lemon rind
pinch of salt
5½ oz/150 g unsalted butter,
chilled and cut into small dice,
plus extra for greasing
1 medium egg, beaten lightly
1 tbsp chilled water

filling

6 oz/175 g unsalted butter,
at room temperature
6 oz/175 g/generous ¾ cup
superfine sugar
3 large eggs
6 oz/175 g/generous 1½ cups
finely ground almonds
2 tsp all-purpose flour
1 tbsp finely grated orange rind
½ tsp almond extract
confectioners' sugar, for dusting
sour cream (optional), to serve

method

1 To make the pie dough, put the flour, sugar, lemon
rind, and salt in a bowl. Rub or cut in the butter until
the mixture resembles fine bread crumbs. Combine
the egg and water, then slowly pour into the flour,
stirring with a fork until a coarse mass forms. Shape
into a ball and let chill for at least 1 hour.

2 Roll out the pie dough on a lightly floured counter
until ⅛ inch/3 mm thick. Use to line a greased 10-inch/
25-cm tart pan. Return to the refrigerator for at least
15 minutes, then cover the tart shell with foil and fill
with dried beans. Place in a preheated oven, 425°F/
220°C, and bake for 12 minutes. Remove the dried
beans and foil and return the tart shell to the oven for
4 minutes to dry the base. Remove from the oven and
reduce the oven temperature to 400°F/200°C.

3 Meanwhile, make the filling. Beat the butter and sugar
until creamy. Beat in the eggs, 1 at a time. Add the
almonds, flour, orange rind, and almond extract, and
beat until blended.

4 Spoon the filling into the tart shell and smooth the
surface. Bake for 30–35 minutes until the top is golden
and the filling is fully baked. Let cool completely on a
wire rack, then dust with sifted confectioners' sugar.
Serve with a spoonful of sour cream, if using.

pear tarte tatin

ingredients

serves 6

6 tbsp butter
4 oz/115 g/generous ½ cup
    superfine sugar
6 pears, peeled, halved,
    and cored
all-purpose flour, for dusting
8 oz/225 g ready-made puff pastry
heavy cream, to serve (optional)

method

1 Melt the butter and sugar in an ovenproof skillet over medium heat. Stir carefully for 5 minutes until it turns to a light caramel color. Take care because it gets very hot.

2 Remove the pan from the heat, place on a heatproof surface, and arrange the pears, cut side up, in the caramel. Place one half in the center and surround it with the others.

3 On a lightly floured counter, roll out the dough to a round, slightly larger than the skillet, and place it on top of the pears. Tuck the edges down into the skillet.

4 Bake near the top of a preheated oven, 400°F/200°C, for 20–25 minutes until the pastry is well risen and golden brown. Remove from the oven and let cool for 2 minutes.

5 Invert the tart onto a serving dish that is larger than the skillet and has enough depth to take any juices that may run out. Remember that this is very hot, so use a pair of thick potholders. Serve warm, with heavy cream if using.

chocolate fudge tart

ingredients

serves 6

12 oz/350 g ready-made
  unsweetened pie dough
flour, for sprinkling
confectioners' sugar, for dusting

filling

5 oz/140 g semisweet chocolate,
  finely chopped
6 oz/175 g butter, diced
12 oz/350 g/1¾ cups golden
  granulated sugar
3½ oz/100 g/¾ cup all-purpose
  flour
½ tsp vanilla extract
6 eggs, beaten

to decorate

5 fl oz/150 ml/⅔ cup whipped
  cream
ground cinnamon

method

1 Roll out the pie dough on a lightly floured counter and
  use to line an 8-inch/20-cm deep loose-bottom tart
  pan. Prick the dough base lightly with a fork, then line
  with foil and fill with dried beans. Bake in a preheated
  oven, 400°F/200°C, for 12–15 minutes, or until the
  dough no longer looks raw. Remove the beans and foil
  and bake for an additional 10 minutes, or until the
  dough is firm. Let cool. Reduce the oven temperature
  to 350°F/180°C.

2 To make the filling, place the chocolate and butter in a
  heatproof bowl and set over a pan of gently simmering
  water until melted. Stir until smooth, then remove
  from the heat and let cool. Place the sugar, flour, vanilla
  extract, and eggs in a separate bowl and whisk until
  well blended. Stir in the chocolate and butter mixture.

3 Pour the filling into the tart shell and bake in the oven
  for 50 minutes, or until the filling is just set. Transfer to
  a wire rack to cool completely. Dust with confectioners'
  sugar before serving with whipped cream sprinkled
  lightly with cinnamon.

toffee apple tart

ingredients
serves 6

butter, for greasing
10 oz/300 g ready-made
    unsweetened pie dough
all-purpose flour, for dusting

filling

3 lb/1.3 kg Pippin or other firm,
    sweet apples, peeled and cored
1 tsp lemon juice
3 heaped tbsp butter
3½ oz/100 g/½ cup superfine
    sugar
7 oz/200 g/1 cup
    granulated sugar
2½ fl oz/75 ml/⅓ cup cold water
5 fl oz/150 ml/⅔ cup heavy cream

method

1 Lightly grease a 9-inch/23-cm loose-bottom fluted tart pan. Roll out the pie dough on a lightly floured counter and line the pan with it, then trim the excess dough. Fit a piece of parchment paper into the tart shell and fill with dried beans. Let chill in the refrigerator for 30 minutes, then bake for 10 minutes in a preheated oven, 375°F/190°C. Remove the beans and paper and return to the oven for 5 minutes.

2 Meanwhile, take 4 apples, cut each one into 8 pieces, and toss in the lemon juice. Melt the butter in a skillet and sauté the apple pieces until just starting to caramelize and brown on the edges. Remove from the skillet and let cool.

3 Slice the remaining apples thinly, put them in a pan with the superfine sugar, and cook for about 20 minutes, until soft. Spoon into the tart shell and arrange the reserved apple pieces on top in a circle. Bake for 30 minutes.

4 Put the granulated sugar and water in a pan and heat until the sugar dissolves. Boil to form a caramel. Remove from the heat and add the cream, stirring constantly to combine into toffee. Remove the tart from the oven, pour the toffee over the apples, and let chill for 1 hour. Serve with heavy cream.

baking with yeast

crusty white bread

ingredients
makes 1 medium loaf

1 egg
1 egg yolk
hand-hot water, as required
1 lb 2 oz/500 g/scant 4 cups
    white bread flour, plus
    extra for dusting
1½ tsp salt
2 tsp sugar
1 tsp active dry yeast
2 tbsp butter, diced
vegetable oil, for oiling

method

1 Place the egg and egg yolk in a pitcher and beat lightly to mix. Add enough hand-hot water to make up to 10 fl oz/300 ml/1¼ cups. Stir well.

2 Place the flour, salt, sugar, and yeast in a large bowl. Add the butter and rub it in until the mixture resembles bread crumbs. Make a well in the center, add the egg mixture, and work to a smooth dough.

3 Turn the dough out and knead for 10 minutes, or until the dough is smooth and elastic. Place the dough in an oiled bowl, cover, and leave in a warm place to rise for 1 hour, or until it has doubled in size.

4 Oil a loaf pan. Turn the dough out onto a lightly floured counter and knead for 1 minute until smooth. Shape the dough to the length of the pan and three times the width. Fold the dough into three lengthwise and place it in the pan with the join underneath. Cover and leave in a warm place for 30 minutes until it has risen above the pan.

5 Bake in a preheated oven, 425°F/220°C, for 30 minutes, or until firm and golden brown. Check the loaf is cooked by tapping it on the bottom—it should sound hollow. Transfer to a wire rack to cool completely.

rye bread

ingredients

makes 1 large loaf

1 lb/450 g/4 cups rye flour

8 oz/225 g/2 cups white bread
flour, plus extra for dusting

2 tsp salt

2 tsp light brown sugar

1½ tsp active dry yeast

15 fl oz/425 ml/scant 2 cups
lukewarm water

2 tsp vegetable oil, plus extra
for brushing

1 egg white

method

1 Sift the flours and salt together into a bowl. Add the sugar and yeast and stir to mix. Make a well in the center and pour in the lukewarm water and oil. Stir until the dough begins to come together, then knead with your hands until it leaves the side of the bowl. Turn out and knead for 10 minutes, until elastic and smooth.

2 Brush a bowl with oil. Shape the dough into a ball, put it into the bowl, and cover with a damp dish towel. Let rise in a warm place for 2 hours, until the dough has doubled in volume. Brush a cookie sheet with oil. Turn out the dough onto a lightly floured counter and punch down with your fist, then knead for 10 minutes. Shape the dough into a ball, put it on the prepared cookie sheet, and cover with a damp dish towel. Let rise in a warm place for 40 minutes, until the dough has doubled in volume.

3 Beat the egg white with 1 tablespoon of water in a bowl. Bake in a preheated oven, 375°F/190°C, for 20 minutes, then remove from the oven and brush the top with the egg white glaze. Return to the oven and bake for an additional 20 minutes. Brush the top of the loaf with the glaze again and return to the oven for 20–30 minutes, until the crust is a rich brown color and the loaf sounds hollow when tapped on the base with your knuckles. Transfer to a wire rack to cool.

plaited poppy seed bread

ingredients

makes 1 loaf

8 oz/225 g/2 cups white bread
flour, plus extra for dusting
1 tsp salt
2 tbsp nonfat dry milk
1½ tbsp superfine sugar
1 tsp active dry yeast
6 fl oz/175 ml/¾ cup lukewarm
water
2 tbsp vegetable oil, plus
extra for brushing
5 tbsp poppy seeds

topping

1 egg yolk
1 tbsp milk
1 tbsp superfine sugar
2 tbsp poppy seeds

method

1 Sift the flour and salt together into a bowl and stir in
the milk, sugar, and yeast. Make a well in the center
and pour in the lukewarm water and oil. Stir well until
the dough begins to come together. Add the poppy
seeds and knead with your hands until they are fully
incorporated. Turn out and knead well for about
10 minutes, until smooth and elastic.

2 Brush a bowl with oil. Shape the dough into a ball,
put it into the bowl, and cover with a damp dish towel.
Let rise in a warm place for 1 hour, until the dough
has doubled in volume. Brush a cookie sheet with oil.
Turn out the dough and knead for 1–2 minutes. Divide
the dough into three equal pieces and shape each into
a rope 10–12 inches/25–30 cm long.

3 Place the ropes side by side and braid the dough.
Pinch the other end together and tuck it underneath.
Put the loaf on the prepared cookie sheet. Cover and
let rise in a warm place for 30 minutes.

4 To make the topping, beat the egg yolk with the milk
and sugar. Brush the egg glaze over the top of the loaf
and sprinkle with the poppy seeds. Bake in a preheated
oven, 400°F/200°C, for 30–35 minutes, until golden
brown and the loaf sounds hollow when tapped with
your knuckles. Transfer to a wire rack to cool.

mixed seed bread

ingredients

makes 1 medium loaf

13 oz/375 g/generous 2½ cups white bread flour, plus extra for dusting

4½ oz/125 g/scant 1½ cups rye flour

1½ tbsp skim milk powder

1½ tsp salt

1 tbsp brown sugar

1 tsp active dry yeast

1½ tbsp sunflower oil, plus extra for oiling

2 tsp lemon juice

10 fl oz/300 ml/1¼ cups hand-hot water

1 tsp caraway seeds

½ tsp poppy seeds

½ tsp sesame seeds

topping

1 egg white

1 tbsp water

1 tbsp sunflower or pumpkin seeds

method

1 Place the flours, milk powder, salt, sugar, and yeast in a bowl. Pour in the oil and add the lemon juice and water Stir in the seeds and mix well to make a smooth dough.

2 Turn the dough out onto a lightly floured counter and knead for 10 minutes, or until the dough is smooth and elastic. Place the dough in an oiled bowl, cover with plastic wrap, and let stand in a warm place to rise for 1 hour, or until it has doubled in size.

3 Oil a 2-lb/900-g loaf pan. Turn the dough out onto a lightly floured counter and knead for 1 minute until smooth. Shape the dough to the length of the pan and three times the width. Fold the dough into three lengthwise and place it in the pan with the join underneath. Cover and let stand in a warm place for 30 minutes until it has risen above the pan.

4 For the topping, lightly beat the egg white with the water to make a glaze. Just before baking, brush the glaze over the loaf, then gently press the sunflower or pumpkin seeds all over the top.

5 Bake in a preheated oven, 425°F/220°C, for 30 minutes, or until firm and golden brown. Test that the loaf is cooked by tapping it on the bottom with your knuckles—it should sound hollow. Transfer to a wire rack to cool completely before serving.

fresh croissants

ingredients

serves 12

1 lb 2 oz/500 g/scant 4 cups white
bread flour, plus extra for
dusting

1½ oz/40 g/scant ¼ cup
superfine sugar

1 tsp salt

2 tsp active dry yeast

10 fl oz/300 ml/1¼ cups milk,
heated until just warm to
the touch

10½ oz/300 g/1¼ cups butter,
softened, flattened with a
rolling pin between 2 sheets
of waxed paper to form a
rectangle ¼ inch/5 mm thick,
then chilled in the refrigerator,
plus extra for greasing

1 egg, lightly beaten with
1 tbsp milk, to glaze

jelly, to serve (optional)

you will need

a cardboard triangular template,
base 7 inches/18 cm and sides
8 inches/20 cm

method

1 Stir the dry ingredients in a large bowl, make a well
in the center, and add the milk. Mix to a soft dough,
adding more milk if too dry. Knead until smooth and
elastic. Let rise in a large, greased bowl, covered, in a
warm place until doubled in size.

2 Knead the dough for 1 minute. Let the butter soften
slightly. Roll out the dough to 18 x 6 inches/46 x 15 cm.
Place the butter in the center. Then with the short end
of the dough toward you, fold the top third down
toward the center, then fold the bottom third up and
squeeze the edges together gently. Rotate so that the
fold is to your left and the top flap toward your right.
Roll out to a rectangle and fold again. If the butter feels
soft, wrap the dough in plastic wrap, and let chill.
Repeat the rolling process twice more. Cut the dough
in half. Roll out one half into a triangle ¼ inch/5 mm
thick (keep the other half refrigerated). Use the
cardboard template to cut out the croissants.

3 Brush the triangles lightly with the glaze. Roll into
croissant shapes, starting at the base and tucking the
point underneath. Brush again with the glaze. Place
on an ungreased cookie sheet and let double in size,
then bake in a preheated oven, 400°F/200°C, for
15–20 minutes until golden. Serve with jelly, if liked.

pains au chocolat

ingredients

serves 8

3½ oz/100 g butter, plus extra
   for greasing
9 oz/250 g/scant 2 cups white
   bread flour, plus extra
   for dusting
1 tsp salt
2 tsp active dry yeast
6 fl oz/175 ml/¾ cup milk
2 tbsp golden superfine sugar
1 tbsp oil, plus extra for brushing
4 oz/115 g semisweet chocolate,
   coarsely chopped

glaze
1 egg yolk
2 tbsp milk

method

1 Grease a cookie sheet. Sift the flour and salt into a bowl and stir in the yeast. Make a well in the center. Heat the milk in a pan until tepid. Add the sugar and oil and stir until the sugar has dissolved. Stir into the flour and mix well. Turn the dough out onto a lightly floured counter and knead until smooth, then place in an oiled bowl. Cover and let rise in a warm place for 2–3 hours, or until doubled in size.

2 Knead on a floured counter and roll into a rectangle 3 times as long as it is wide. Divide the butter into thirds. Dot one portion over the top two-thirds of the dough, leaving a ½-inch/1-cm margin round the edges. Fold the lower third up and the top third down. Seal the edges. Give the dough a half-turn. Roll into a rectangle. Repeat the process twice, then fold in half. Put into an oiled plastic bag. Let chill for 1 hour.

3 Cut the dough in half and roll out into 2 rectangles of 12 x 6 inches/30 x 15 cm. Cut each half into 4 rectangles of 6 x 3 inches/15 x 7.5 cm. Sprinkle chocolate along one short end of each and roll up. Place on the cookie sheet in a warm place for 2–3 hours, or until doubled in size. To glaze, mix the egg yolk and milk and brush over the rolls. Bake in a preheated oven, 425°F/220°C, for 15–20 minutes, or until golden and well risen.

stollen

ingredients

serves 10

3 oz/85 g/generous ½ cup currants
2 oz/55 g/⅓ cup raisins
2 tbsp chopped candied peel
2 oz/55 g/⅓ cup candied cherries,
    rinsed, dried, and quartered
2 tbsp rum
2 oz/55 g butter
6 fl oz/175 ml/¾ cup milk
2 tbsp golden superfine sugar
13 oz/375 g/generous 2¾ cups
    strong white bread flour, plus
    extra for dusting
½ tsp ground nutmeg
½ tsp ground cinnamon
seeds from 3 cardamoms
2 tsp active dry yeast
finely grated rind of 1 lemon
1 egg, beaten
1½ oz/40 g/scant ½ cup
    slivered almonds
vegetable oil, for brushing
6 oz/175 g marzipan
melted butter, for brushing
sifted confectioners' sugar,
    for dredging

method

1 Place the currants, raisins, peel, and cherries in a bowl, stir in the rum and set aside. Place the butter, milk, and sugar in a pan over low heat and stir until the sugar dissolves and the butter melts. Cool until lukewarm. Sift the flour, nutmeg, and cinnamon into a bowl. Crush the cardamom seeds and add them. Stir in the yeast. Make a well in the center, stir in the milk mixture, lemon rind, and egg and beat into a dough.

2 Turn the dough out onto a floured counter. Knead for 5 minutes, adding more flour if necessary. Knead in the soaked fruit and the almonds. Transfer to a clean, oiled bowl. Cover with plastic wrap and let stand in a warm place for up to 3 hours, or until doubled in size. Turn out onto a floured counter, knead for 1–2 minutes, then roll out to a 10-inch/25-cm square.

3 Roll the marzipan into a sausage shape, shorter than the length of the dough. Place in the center. Fold the dough over the marzipan, overlapping it. Seal the ends Place seam-side down on a greased cookie sheet, cover with oiled plastic wrap, and let stand in a warm place for up to 2 hours, or until doubled in size. Bake in a preheated over, 375°F/190°C, for 40 minutes, or until golden and hollow sounding when tapped. Brush with melted butter, dredge with confectioners' sugar, and let cool on a wire rack.

apricot & walnut bread

ingredients

serves 12

2 oz/55 g butter, plus extra
    for greasing
12 oz/350 g/generous 2½ cups
    strong white bread flour, plus
    extra for dusting
½ tsp salt
1 tsp golden superfine sugar
2 tsp active dry yeast
4 oz/115 g/generous ⅔ cup
    no-soak dried apricots,
    chopped
2 oz/55 g/⅓ cup chopped walnuts
5 fl oz/150 ml/⅔ cup tepid milk
2½ fl oz/75 ml/scant ⅓ cup
    tepid water
1 egg, beaten
vegetable oil, for brushing

topping

3 oz/85 g/generous ¾ cup
    confectioners' sugar
a little water
walnut halves

method

1 Grease and flour a cookie sheet. Sift the flour and salt into a warmed bowl and stir in the sugar and yeast. Rub in the butter and add the chopped apricots and walnuts. Make a well in the center. In a separate bowl, mix together the milk, water, and egg. Pour into the dry ingredients and mix to a soft dough. Turn out onto a floured counter and knead for 10 minutes, or until smooth. Place the dough in a clean bowl brushed with oil, cover with oiled plastic wrap, and let stand in a warm place for 2–3 hours, or until doubled in size.

2 Turn the dough out onto a floured counter and knead lightly for 1 minute. Divide into 5 equal pieces and roll each piece into a rope 12-inches/30-cm long. Braid 3 ropes together, pinching the ends to seal, and place on the prepared cookie sheet. Twist the remaining 2 ropes together and place on top. Cover lightly with oiled plastic wrap and let stand in a warm place for 1–2 hours, or until doubled in size.

3 Bake the bread in a preheated oven, 425°F/220°C, for 10 minutes, then reduce the heat to 375°F/190°C, and bake for an additional 20 minutes. Transfer to a wire rack to cool. To make the topping, sift the confectioners' sugar into a bowl, stir in enough water to make a thin frosting and drizzle over the loaf. Decorate with walnut halves and serve.

orange & raisin brioches

ingredients

serves 12

2 oz/55 g butter, melted,
    plus extra for greasing
8 oz/225 g/generous 1½ cups
    strong white bread flour,
    plus extra for dusting
½ tsp salt
2 tsp active dry yeast
1 tbsp golden superfine sugar
2 oz/55 g/⅓ cup raisins
grated rind of 1 orange
2 tbsp tepid water
2 eggs, beaten
vegetable oil, for oiling
1 beaten egg, for glazing
butter, to serve (optional)

method

1 Grease 12 individual brioche molds. Sift the flour and salt into a warmed bowl and stir in the yeast, sugar, raisins, and orange rind. Make a well in the center. In a separate bowl, mix together the water, eggs, and melted butter and pour into the dry ingredients. Beat vigorously to make a soft dough. Turn out and knead for 5 minutes, or until smooth and elastic. Brush a clean bowl with oil. Place the dough in the bowl, cover with plastic wrap, and let stand in a warm place for 1 hour, or until doubled in size.

2 Turn out onto a floured counter, knead lightly for 1 minute, then roll into a rope shape. Cut into 12 equal pieces. Shape three-fourths of each piece into a ball and place in the prepared molds. With a floured finger, press a hole in the center of each. Shape the remaining pieces of dough into little plugs and press into the holes, flattening the top slightly.

3 Place the molds on a cookie sheet, cover lightly with oiled plastic wrap, and let stand in a warm place for 1 hour, until the dough comes almost to the top.

4 Brush the brioches with beaten egg and bake in a preheated oven, 425°F/220°C, for 15 minutes, or until golden brown. Serve warm with butter, if you like.

date & honey loaf

ingredients

serves 10

butter, for greasing

9 oz/250 g/1¾ cups strong white bread flour, plus extra for dusting

2¾ oz/75 g/½ cup strong brown bread flour

½ tsp salt

¼-oz/7-g envelope active dry yeast

7 fl oz/200 ml/scant 1 cup lukewarm water

3 tbsp corn oil

3 tbsp honey

2¾ oz/75 g/½ cup dried dates, chopped

2 tbsp sesame seeds

method

1 Grease a 2-lb/900-g loaf pan with butter. Sift the white and brown flours into a large bowl and stir in the salt and yeast. Pour in the water, oil, and honey and mix to form a dough.

2 Place the dough on a lightly floured counter and knead for 5 minutes, or until smooth, then place in a greased bowl. Cover and let rise in a warm place for 1 hour, or until doubled in size.

3 Knead in the dates and sesame seeds. Shape the dough and place in the prepared pan. Cover and let stand in a warm place for an additional 30 minutes, or until springy to the touch.

4 Bake the loaf in a preheated oven, 425°F/220°C, for 30 minutes, or until the bottom of the loaf sounds hollow when tapped. Transfer to a wire rack and let cool completely. Serve cut into thick slices.

mango twist bread

ingredients

makes 1 loaf

3 tbsp butter, diced, plus extra
  for greasing
1 lb/450 g/3½ cups strong white
  bread flour, plus extra
  for dusting
1 tsp salt
1 envelope active dry yeast
1 tsp ground ginger
1¾ oz/50 g/¼ cup brown sugar
1 small mango, peeled, pitted,
  and blended to a paste
9 fl oz/250 ml/1 cup
  lukewarm water
2 tbsp honey
4½ oz/125 g/⅔ cup golden raisins
1 egg, beaten lightly
confectioners' sugar, for dusting

method

1 Grease a cookie sheet with a little butter. Sift the flour and salt into a mixing bowl, stir in the dry yeast, ginger, and brown sugar and rub in the butter with your fingertips until the mixture resembles bread crumbs.

2 Stir in the mango paste, lukewarm water, and honey and bring together to form a dough.

3 Place the dough on a lightly floured counter. Knead for about 5 minutes, until smooth. Alternatively, use an electric mixer with a dough hook. Place the dough in a greased bowl, cover, and let rise in a warm place for about 1 hour, until it has doubled in size.

4 Knead in the golden raisins and shape the dough into 2 rope shapes, each 10 inches/25 cm long. Carefully twist the 2 pieces together and pinch the ends to seal. Place the dough on the cookie sheet, cover, and let stand in a warm place for an additional 40 minutes.

5 Brush the loaf with the egg. Bake in a preheated oven, 425°F/220°C, for 30 minutes, or until golden. Let cool on a wire rack and dust with confectioners' sugar before serving.

black olive focaccia

ingredients

serves 12

1 lb 2 oz/500 g/scant 4 cups
  strong white bread flour,
  plus extra for dusting
1 tsp salt
2 tsp active dry yeast
12 fl oz/350 ml/1½ cups tepid
  water
6 tbsp extra-virgin olive oil,
  plus extra for oiling
4 oz/115 g/⅔ cup pitted black
  olives, coarsely chopped
1 tsp rock salt

method

1 Sift the flour and salt into a warmed bowl and stir in
  the yeast. Pour in the water and 2 tablespoons of the
  olive oil and mix to a soft dough. Knead the dough
  on a lightly floured counter for 5–10 minutes, or until
  it becomes smooth and elastic. Transfer it to a clean,
  warmed, oiled bowl and cover with plastic wrap. Let
  stand in a warm place for 1 hour, or until the dough
  has doubled in size.

2 Brush 2 cookie sheets with oil. Punch the dough to
  knock out the air, then knead on a lightly floured
  counter for 1 minute. Add the olives and knead until
  combined. Divide the dough in half and shape into
  2 oval shapes 11 x 9 inches/28 x 23 cm long, and place
  on the prepared cookie sheets. Cover with oiled plastic
  wrap and let stand in a warm place for 1 hour, or until
  the dough is puffy.

3 Press your fingers into the dough to make dimples,
  drizzle over 2 tablespoons of oil, and sprinkle with
  the rock salt. Bake in a preheated oven, 400°F/200°C,
  for 30–35 minutes, or until golden. Drizzle with the
  remaining olive oil and cover with a cloth, to give a
  soft crust. Slice each loaf into 6 pieces and serve warm.

focaccia with roasted cherry tomatoes, basil & crispy pancetta

ingredients

serves 4–6

1 lb 2 oz/500 g/scant 4 cups white bread flour, plus extra for kneading and rolling, and for dusting

1 tbsp dried basil

½ tsp sugar

2 tsp rapid-rise dried yeast

2 tsp salt

11 fl oz/325 ml/generous 1¼ cups water, lukewarm

2 tbsp olive oil, plus extra for oiling

topping

14 oz/400 g cherry tomatoes

1 tbsp olive oil, plus extra for oiling and drizzling

salt and pepper

7 oz/200 g thick pancetta, diced

4 tbsp chopped fresh basil

method

1 Place the flour, dried basil, sugar, yeast, and salt in a bowl. Combine the water and oil and mix with the dry ingredients to form a soft dough, adding more water if the dough appears too dry. Turn out onto a lightly floured counter and knead for 10 minutes, or until the dough is smooth and elastic. Place in a lightly oiled bowl and cover with plastic wrap. Let stand in a warm place for 1 hour, or until doubled in size.

2 Place the tomatoes on a cookie sheet covered with parchment paper, sprinkle with oil, and season with salt and pepper. Bake in a preheated oven, 275°F/140°C, for 30 minutes, or until the tomatoes are soft.

3 Increase the oven temperature to 425°F/220°C. Remove the dough from the bowl and knead again briefly. Shape into a rectangle and place on a lightly oiled cookie sheet, turning the dough over to oil both sides. Make rough indentations in the dough using your fingers. Top with the tomatoes and pancetta. Sprinkle with salt and pepper. Let stand in a warm place for 10 minutes for the dough to rise again. Bake for 15–20 minutes, or until golden brown and cooked through. Drizzle with oil and top with fresh basil. Serve warm.

olive & sun-dried tomato bread

ingredients

serves 4

14 oz/400 g/generous 2¾ cups
   all-purpose flour, plus extra
   for dusting
1 tsp salt
1 envelope active dry yeast
1 tsp brown sugar
1 tbsp chopped fresh thyme
7 fl oz/200 ml/scant 1 cup warm
   water (heated to 122°F/50°C)
1¾ oz/50 g/⅓ cup black olives,
   pitted and sliced
4 tbsp olive oil, plus
   extra for oiling
1¾ oz/50 g/⅓ cup green olives,
   pitted and sliced
3½ oz/100 g/scant ½ cup
   sun-dried tomatoes in oil,
   drained and sliced
1 egg yolk, beaten

method

1 Place the flour, salt, and yeast in a bowl and mix
   together, then stir in the sugar and thyme. Make a well
   in the center. Slowly stir in enough warm water and
   oil to make a dough. Mix in the olives and sun-dried
   tomatoes. Knead the dough for 5 minutes, then form it
   into a ball. Brush a bowl with oil, add the dough, and
   cover with plastic wrap. Let rise in a warm place for
   about 1½ hours, or until it has doubled in size.

2 Dust a cookie sheet with flour. Knead the dough lightly,
   then cut into two halves and shape into ovals or circles.
   Place them on the cookie sheet, cover with plastic
   wrap, and let rise again in a warm place for 45 minutes,
   or until they have doubled in size.

3 Make 3 shallow diagonal cuts on the top of each piece
   of dough. Brush with the egg. Bake in a preheated
   oven, 400°F/200°C, for 40 minutes, or until cooked
   through—they should be golden on top and sound
   hollow when tapped on the bottom. Transfer to wire
   racks to cool. Store in an airtight container for up to
   3 days.

cheese & chive plait

ingredients

serves 10

1 lb/450 g/3½ cups strong white
    bread flour, plus extra for
    dusting
1 tsp salt
1 tsp superfine sugar
1½ tsp active dry yeast
2 tbsp butter
4 oz/115 g/generous 1 cup
    coarsely grated Cheddar cheese
3 tbsp snipped fresh chives
4 scallions, chopped
5 fl oz/150 ml/⅔ cup tepid milk
6 fl oz/175 ml/¾ cup tepid water
vegetable oil, for oiling
beaten egg, for glazing

method

1 Sift the flour and salt into a warmed bowl and stir in
the sugar and yeast. Rub in the butter, then stir in
the cheese, chives, and scallions. Make a well in the
center. Mix together the milk and water, pour into the
well, and mix to make a soft dough. Turn the dough
out onto a lightly floured counter and knead for
10 minutes, or until smooth and elastic.

2 Transfer the dough to a clean, oiled bowl and cover
with plastic wrap. Let stand in a warm place for 1 hour,
or until doubled in size. Brush a large cookie sheet
with oil. Turn the dough out onto a floured counter
and knead for 1 minute. Divide the dough into 3 pieces.
Roll out each piece into a rope shape and braid the
3 pieces together, pinching the ends to seal.

3 Place on the prepared cookie sheet and cover with
oiled plastic wrap. Let stand in a warm place for
45 minutes, or until doubled in size. Brush with beaten
egg and bake in a preheated oven, 425°F/220°C, for
20 minutes.

4 Reduce the oven temperature to 350°F/180°C and
bake for an additional 15 minutes, or until golden
brown and the loaf sounds hollow when tapped on
the bottom. Serve warm or cold.

turkish flatbread

ingredients

serves 8

1 lb 10 oz/750 g/6½ cups
all-purpose flour,
plus extra for dusting
1½ tsp salt
1 tsp ground cumin
½ tsp ground coriander
1 tsp superfine sugar
¼ oz/7 g active dry yeast
2 tbsp olive oil, plus extra
for brushing
14 fl oz/400 ml/1¾ cups
lukewarm water

method

1 Sift together the flour, salt, cumin, and coriander into a bowl and stir in the sugar and yeast. Make a well in the center and pour in the oil and lukewarm water. Stir well with a wooden spoon until the dough begins to come together, then knead with your hands until it leaves the side of the bowl. Turn out and knead well for about 10 minutes, until smooth and elastic.

2 Brush a bowl with oil. Shape the dough into a ball, put it into the bowl, and cover with a damp dish towel. Let rise in a warm place for 1 hour, until the dough has doubled in volume.

3 Lightly brush a cookie sheet with oil. Turn out the dough onto a lightly floured counter, punch down with your fist, and knead for 1–2 minutes. Divide the dough into eight equal pieces, shape each piece into a ball, then roll out to an 8-inch/20-cm round. Cover the rounds with a damp dish towel and let rest for 20 minutes.

4 Heat a heavy skillet and brush the bottom with oil. Add one of the dough rounds, cover, and cook for 2–3 minutes, until lightly browned on the underside. Turn over with a metal spatula, re-cover the skillet, and cook for an additional 2 minutes, until lightly browned on the second side. Remove from the skillet and cook the remaining dough rounds in the same way.

cilantro & garlic naan

ingredients

serves 3

10 oz/280 g/2½ cups white bread
   flour, plus extra for dusting
1 tsp salt
1 tbsp ground coriander
1 garlic clove, very finely chopped
1 tsp active dry yeast
2 tsp honey
3½ fl oz/100 ml/scant ½ cup
   lukewarm water
4 tbsp plain yogurt
1 tbsp vegetable oil, plus extra
   for brushing
1 tsp black onion seeds
1 tbsp chopped fresh cilantro

method

1 Sift the flour, salt, and coriander together into a bowl
   and stir in the garlic and yeast. Make a well in the
   center and pour in the honey, lukewarm water, yogurt,
   and oil. Stir well until the dough comes together, then
   knead with your hands until it leaves the side of the
   bowl. Turn out onto a lightly floured counter and knead
   well for about 10 minutes, until smooth and elastic.

2 Brush a bowl with oil. Shape the dough into a ball, put
   it into the bowl, and cover with a damp dish towel. Let
   rise in a warm place for 1–2 hours, until the dough has
   doubled in volume. Prepare three cookie sheets and
   place in a preheated oven, 475°F/240°C. Turn out the
   dough onto a lightly floured counter and punch down
   with your fist. Divide the dough into three pieces,
   shape each piece into a ball, and cover two of them
   with oiled plastic wrap. Roll out the uncovered piece of
   dough into a teardrop shape about ³⁄₈ inch/8 mm thick
   and cover with oiled plastic wrap. Roll out the other
   pieces of dough in the same way.

3 Place the naans on the preheated cookie sheets and
   sprinkle with the onion seeds and chopped cilantro.
   Bake in the preheated oven for 5 minutes, until puffed
   up. Transfer the naans to the broiler pan, brush with oil,
   and broil for 2–3 minutes. Serve warm.

bagels

ingredients

serves 10

12 oz/350 g/3 cups white bread
flour, plus extra for dusting
2 tsp salt
¼ oz/7 g active dry yeast
1 tbsp lightly beaten egg
7 fl oz/200 ml/scant 1 cup
lukewarm water
vegetable oil, for brushing
1 egg white
2 tsp water
2 tbsp caraway seeds

method

1 Sift the flour and salt together into a bowl and stir in
the yeast. Make a well in the center, pour in the egg
and lukewarm water, and mix to a dough. Turn out
and knead well for about 10 minutes, until smooth.

2 Brush a bowl with oil. Shape the dough into a ball,
place it in the bowl. Cover and let rise in a warm place
for 1 hour, until the dough has doubled in volume.
Brush two cookie sheets with oil and dust a baking
sheet with flour. Turn out the dough onto a lightly
floured counter. Knead for 2 minutes, then divide into
ten pieces. Shape each piece into a ball and let rest for
5 minutes. Gently flatten each ball and make a hole in
the center with the handle of a wooden spoon. Put the
bagels on the floured sheet, cover with a damp dish
towel, and let rise in a warm place for 20 minutes.

3 Bring a large saucepan of water to a boil. Reduce the
heat until the water is barely simmering, then add two
bagels. Poach for 1 minute, then turn over, and poach
for 30 seconds more. Poach the others in the same way.

4 Transfer the bagels to the oiled cookie sheets. Beat the
egg white with the water in a bowl and brush it over
the bagels. Sprinkle with the caraway seeds and bake
in a preheated oven, 425°F/220°C for 25–30 minutes,
until golden brown. Transfer to a wire rack to cool.

english muffins

ingredients

serves 10–12

2 x ¼-oz/7-g envelopes
     active dry yeast
9 fl oz/250 ml/1 cup tepid water
4 fl oz/125 ml/½ cup natural
     yogurt
1 lb/450 g/3½ cups strong
     plain flour
½ tsp salt
1¾ oz/50 g/¼ cup fine semolina
oil, for greasing
butter and jelly (optional), to serve

method

1 Mix the yeast with half the tepid water in a bowl until it
   has dissolved. Add the remaining water and the yogurt
   and mix well.

2 Sift the flour into a large bowl and add the salt. Pour
   in the yeast liquid and mix well to a soft dough. Turn
   out onto a floured counter and knead well until very
   smooth. Put the dough back into the bowl, cover with
   plastic wrap, and let rise for 30–40 minutes in a warm
   place until it has doubled in size.

3 Turn out again onto the counter and knead lightly.
   Roll out the dough to a thickness of ¾ inch/2 cm.
   Using a 3-inch/7.5-cm cutter, cut into rounds and
   scatter the semolina over each muffin. Re-roll the
   trimmings of the dough and make further muffins
   until all the dough is used up. Place them on a lightly
   floured baking sheet, cover, and let rise again
   for 30–40 minutes.

4 Heat a large skillet and lightly grease with a little oil.
   Cook half the muffins for 7–8 minutes on each side,
   taking care not to burn them. Repeat with the rest
   of the muffins. Serve at once with lots of butter and
   jelly, if liked.

cheese & tomato pizza

ingredients

serves 2

dough

8 oz/225 g/1½ cups all-purpose
    flour, plus extra for dusting
1 tsp salt
1 tsp active dry yeast
1 tbsp olive oil, plus extra for oiling
6 tbsp lukewarm water

topping

6 tomatoes, sliced thinly
6 oz/175 g mozzarella cheese,
    drained and sliced thinly
salt and pepper
2 tbsp shredded fresh basil leaves
2 tbsp olive oil

method

1 To make the pizza dough, sift the flour and salt into a bowl and stir in the yeast. Make a well in the center and pour in the oil and water. Gradually incorporate the dry ingredients into the liquid, using a wooden spoon or floured hands.

2 Turn out the dough onto a lightly floured counter and knead well for 5 minutes, until smooth and elastic. Return to the clean bowl, cover with lightly oiled plastic wrap, and set aside to rise in a warm place for about 1 hour, or until doubled in size.

3 Turn out the dough onto a lightly floured counter and knock down. Knead briefly, then cut it in half and roll out each piece into a circle about ¼ inch/5 mm thick. Transfer to a lightly oiled cookie sheet and push up the edges with your fingers to form a small rim.

4 For the topping, arrange the tomato and mozzarella slices alternately over the pizza bases. Season to taste with salt and pepper, sprinkle with the basil, and drizzle with the olive oil. Bake in a preheated oven, 450°F/230°C, for 15–20 minutes, until the crust is crisp and the cheese has melted. Serve immediately.

blinis

ingredients

serves 8

4 oz/115 g/¾ cup buckwheat flour
4 oz/115 g/¾ cup white bread flour
¼-oz/7-g envelope active
    dry yeast
1 tsp salt
13 fl oz/375 ml/scant 1¾ cups
    tepid milk
2 eggs, 1 whole and 1 separated
vegetable oil, for brushing
sour cream and smoked salmon,
    to serve

method

1 Sift both flours into a large, warmed bowl. Stir in the yeast and salt. Beat in the milk, whole egg, and egg yolk until smooth. Cover the bowl and let stand in a warm place for 1 hour.

2 Place the egg white in a spotlessly clean bowl and whisk until soft peaks form. Fold into the batter. Brush a heavy-bottom skillet with oil and set over medium–high heat. When the skillet is hot, pour enough of the batter onto the surface to make a blini about the size of a saucer.

3 When bubbles rise, turn the blini over with a spatula and cook the other side until light brown. Wrap in a clean dish towel to keep warm while cooking the remainder. Serve the warm blinis with sour cream and smoked salmon.

savory
nibbles

savory oat crackers

ingredients

makes 12–14

3½ oz/100 g unsalted butter,
    plus extra for greasing
3½ oz/90 g/scant 1 cup rolled oats
¼ cup whole wheat flour
½ tsp coarse salt
1 tsp dried thyme
1½ oz/40 g/⅓ cup walnuts,
    finely chopped
1 egg, beaten
3 tbsp sesame seeds

method

1 Lightly grease two cookie sheets.

2 Rub the butter into the oats and flour using your fingertips. Stir in the salt, thyme, and walnuts, then add the egg and mix to a soft dough. Break off walnut-size pieces of dough and roll into balls, then roll in sesame seeds to coat lightly and evenly.

3 Place the balls of dough on the prepared cookie sheets, spacing them well apart, and roll the rolling pin over them to flatten as much as possible. Bake in a preheated oven, 350°F/180°C for 12–15 minutes, or until firm and pale golden in color.

4 Cool on the cookie sheets for 3–4 minutes, then transfer to a wire rack to finish cooling.

cheese & mustard scones

ingredients

serves 8

1¹/₂ oz/50 g butter, cut into small
  pieces, plus extra for greasing
8 oz/225 g/generous 1¹/₂ cups
  self-rising flour, plus extra
  for dusting
1 tsp baking powder
pinch of salt
4¹/₂ oz/105 g/1¹/₂ cups grated
  sharp Cheddar cheese
1 tsp mustard powder
5 fl oz/150 ml/²/₃ cup milk, plus
  extra for brushing
pepper

method

1 Lightly grease a cookie sheet.

2 Sift the flour, baking powder, and salt into a mixing
  bowl. Rub in the butter with your fingertips until the
  mixture resembles breadcrumbs.

3 Stir in the cheese, mustard, and enough milk to form
  a soft dough.

4 On a lightly floured counter, knead the dough very
  lightly, then flatten it out with the palm of your hand
  to a depth of about 1 inch/2.5 cm.

5 Cut the dough into eight wedges with a knife. Brush
  each one with a little milk and sprinkle with pepper
  to taste.

6 Bake in a preheated oven, 425°F/220°C, for 10–15
  minutes, until golden brown. Transfer the scones to
  a wire rack and let cool slightly before serving.

quiche lorraine

ingredients

serves 4

pie dough

7 oz/200 g/1¾ cups all-purpose
   flour, plus extra for dusting
3½ oz/100 g/scant ½ cup butter
1–2 tbsp cold water

filling

½ oz/15 g butter
1 small onion, finely chopped
4 lean bacon strips, diced
2 oz/55 g/½ cup grated Gruyère
   cheese or Cheddar cheese
2 eggs, beaten
10 fl oz/300 ml/1¼ cups light
   cream
pepper

method

1 For the pie dough, sift the flour into a bowl and rub
   in the butter with your fingertips until the mixture
   resembles fine breadcrumbs. Stir in just enough water
   to bind the mixture to a firm dough.

2 Roll out the dough on a lightly floured counter to a
   round slightly larger than a 9-inch/23-cm loose-bottom
   round tart pan, 1¼ inches/3 cm deep. Lift the dough
   onto the pan and press it down into the fluted edge.
   Trim off the excess dough. Prick the bottom with a fork.
   Chill to let the dough rest and prevent shrinkage.

3 Place parchment paper in the pie shell. Fill with dried
   beans to weigh it down. Place on the baking sheet and
   bake in a preheated oven, 400°F/200°C, for 10 minutes.
   Remove the paper and beans and bake for 10 minutes.

4 For the filling, melt the butter in a skillet and cook
   the onion and bacon until soft. Spread the mixture
   in the hot pie shell and sprinkle with half the cheese.
   Beat together the eggs and cream and season to taste.
   Pour into the pie shell and sprinkle with cheese.

5 Reduce the oven temperature to 375°F/190°C. Place
   the quiche in the oven and bake for 25–30 minutes, or
   until golden brown and just set. Let cool for 10 minute
   before turning out.

goat cheese & thyme tart

ingredients

serves 6

9 oz/250 g ready-made puff pastry

topping

1 lb 2 oz/500 g goat cheese,
    such as chèvre, sliced
3–4 sprigs fresh thyme, leaves
    picked from stalks
2 oz/55 g/scant ⅓ cup black
    olives, pitted
1¾ oz/50 g tinned anchovies
    in olive oil
1 tbsp olive oil
salt and pepper
1 egg yolk
fresh sprigs of thyme, to garnish

method

1 Roll the dough into a large circle or rectangle and place on a baking sheet.

2 Arrange the cheese slices on the dough, leaving a 1-inch/2.5-cm margin round the edge. Sprinkle the thyme and olives, then arrange the anchovies, over the cheese. Drizzle over the olive oil. Season well with salt and pepper and brush the edges of the dough with the egg yolk.

3 Bake in a preheated oven, 375°F/190°C, for 20–25 minutes, until the cheese is bubbling and the pastry is browned. Garnish with fresh sprigs of thyme.

crab & watercress tart

ingredients

serves 6

pie dough

4½ oz/125 g/generous ¾ cup
    all-purpose flour
pinch of salt
2½ oz/75 g cold butter,
    cut into pieces
cold water

filling

10½ oz/300 g prepared white
    and brown crabmeat
1 bunch watercress, washed and
    leaves picked from stems
2 fl oz/50 ml/¼ cup milk
2 large eggs, plus 3 egg yolks
7 fl oz/200 ml/scant 1 cup
    heavy cream
salt and pepper
½ tsp ground nutmeg
½ bunch fresh chives, snipped
2 tbsp finely grated Parmesan
    cheese
fresh sprigs of watercress,
    to garnish

method

1 Lightly grease a 9-inch/23-cm loose-bottom fluted tart pan. Sift the flour and salt into a food processor, add the butter, and process until the mixture resembles fine bread crumbs. Add just enough cold water to bring the dough together.

2 Turn out and roll out the dough 3¼ inches/8 cm larger than the pan. Carefully lift the dough into the pan and press to fit. Neaten the edges and trim the excess dough. Fit a piece of parchment paper into the tart shell, fill with dried beans, and let chill for 30 minutes.

3 Remove the pastry shell from the refrigerator and bake blind for 10 minutes in a preheated oven, 375°F/190°C, then remove the beans and paper. Return to the oven for 5 minutes. Remove the pan from the oven and lower the oven temperature to 325°F/160°C.

4 Arrange the crabmeat and watercress in the tart pan. Whisk the milk, eggs, and egg yolks together in a bowl. Bring the cream to simmering point in a pan and pour over the egg mixture, whisking all the time. Season with salt, pepper, and nutmeg and stir in the chives. Carefully pour this mixture over the crab and watercress and sprinkle over the Parmesan. Bake for 35–40 minutes, until golden and set. Let the tart stand for 10 minutes before serving with sprigs of watercress.

triple tomato tart

ingredients

serves 6

all-purpose flour, for dusting
9 oz/250 g ready-made puff pastry

topping

3 tbsp sundried tomato paste
9 oz/250 g ripe vine tomatoes,
 sliced
5½ oz/150 g cherry tomatoes,
 cut in half
2 sprigs fresh rosemary
2 tbsp extra-virgin olive oil
1 tbsp balsamic vinegar
1 egg yolk
4½ oz/125 g Italian sliced salami,
 chopped
salt and pepper
handful thyme sprigs

method

1 On a lightly floured counter, roll out the dough to form a rectangle 14 inches/36 cm long and 10 inches/25 cm wide and lift onto a heavy-duty cookie sheet. Spread the sundried tomato paste over the dough, leaving a 1¼-inch/3-cm margin round the edge. Arrange the vine tomato slices over the tomato paste, sprinkle over the cherry tomato halves and top with the rosemary. Drizzle with 1 tablespoon of the olive oil and the balsamic vinegar.

2 Brush the edges of the dough with the egg yolk and bake in a preheated oven, 375°F/190°C, for 10 minutes. Sprinkle over the chopped salami and bake for an additional 10–15 minutes.

3 Remove the tart from the oven and season with salt and pepper. Drizzle with the remaining olive oil and sprinkle with the thyme.

spring vegetable tart

ingredients

serves 6

pie dough

9 oz/250 g/1¾ cups
    all-purpose flour
pinch of salt
4½ oz/125 g cold butter,
    cut into pieces
2 oz/55 g/½ cup grated Parmesan
    cheese
1 egg
cold water

filling

11 oz/300 g selection of baby
    spring vegetables, such as
    carrots, asparagus, peas, fava
    beans, scallions, corn cobs, and
    leeks, trimmed and peeled
    where necessary
10 fl oz/300 ml/1¼ cups
    heavy cream
4½ oz/125 g sharp Cheddar
    cheese, grated
2 eggs plus 3 egg yolks
salt and pepper
handful fresh tarragon and flatleaf
    parsley, chopped

method

1 Grease a 10-inch/25-cm loose-bottom tart pan. Sift the flour and salt into a food processor, add the butter, and pulse to combine, then tip into a large bowl and add the Parmesan cheese. Mix the egg and water together in a small bowl. Add most of the egg mixture and work into a soft dough. Roll out the dough 3¼ inches/8 cm larger than the pan. Carefully lift the dough into the pan and press to fit. Trim the excess dough. Fit a piece of parchment paper into the tart shell, fill with dried beans, and let chill in the refrigerator for 30 minutes.

2 Bake the tart shell blind for 15 minutes in a preheated oven, 400°F/200°C, then remove the beans and paper and bake for an additional 5 minutes. Remove from the oven and let cool. Lower the oven temperature to 350°F/180°C.

3 Cut the vegetables into bite-size pieces and blanch in boiling water. Drain and let cool. Bring the cream to simmering point in a pan. Place the cheese, eggs, and egg yolks in a heatproof bowl and pour the warm cream over the mixture. Stir to combine, season well, and stir in the herbs. Arrange the vegetables in the tart shell, pour over the cheese filling, and bake for 30–40 minutes, until set. Let cool in the pan for 10 minutes before serving.

yellow zucchini tart

ingredients

serves 6

butter, for greasing
9 oz/250 g ready-made pie dough,
    thawed if frozen
all-purpose flour, for dusting

filling

2 large yellow zucchini
1 tbsp salt
3 heaped tbsp unsalted butter
1 bunch scallions, trimmed and
    finely sliced
5 fl oz/150 ml/²/₃ cup heavy cream
3 large eggs
fresh chives, chopped, plus extra
    to garnish
salt and white pepper

method

1 Grease a 10-inch/25-cm loose-bottom tart pan. On a lightly floured counter, roll out the pie dough 3¼ inches/8 cm larger than the pan. Carefully lift the dough into the pan and press to fit. Roll the rolling pin over the pan to neaten the edges and trim the excess dough. Fit a piece of parchment paper into the tart shell, fill with dried beans, and let chill in the refrigerator for 30 minutes.

2 Bake the tart shell blind for 15 minutes in a preheated oven, 400°F/200°C, then remove the beans and paper and bake for an additional 5 minutes. Remove from the oven and let cool. Lower the oven temperature to 350°F/180°C.

3 Meanwhile, grate the zucchini and put in a strainer with 1 tablespoon of salt. Let drain for 20 minutes, then rinse and put in a clean dish towel, squeezing all the moisture from the zucchini. Keep dry.

4 Melt the butter in a wide skillet, sauté the scallions until soft, then add the zucchini and cook for 5 minutes, until any liquid has evaporated. Let cool slightly. Whisk together the cream, eggs, salt, pepper, and chives. Spoon the zucchini into the tart shell and pour in the mixture, then bake for 30 minutes. Serve tart hot or cold, garnished with fresh chives.

squash, sage & gorgonzola tart

ingredients

serves 6

butter, for greasing
9 oz/250 g ready-made pie dough,
    thawed if frozen
all-purpose flour, for dusting

filling

½ small butternut squash or
    1 slice pumpkin, weighing
    9 oz/250 g
1 tsp olive oil
9 fl oz/250 ml/generous 1 cup
    heavy cream
salt and pepper
6 oz/175 g Gorgonzola cheese
2 eggs, plus 1 egg yolk
6–8 fresh sage leaves

method

1 Cut the squash in half and brush the cut side with the oil. Place cut-side up on a cookie sheet and bake for 30–40 minutes, until browned and very soft. Let cool. Remove the seeds and scoop out the flesh into a large bowl, discarding the skin.

2 Lightly grease a 9-inch/22-cm loose-bottom fluted tart pan. On a lightly floured counter, roll out the pie dough 3¼ inches/8 cm larger than the pan. Lift the dough into the pan and press to fit. Trim the excess dough. Fit a piece of parchment paper into the tart shell and fill it with dried beans. Let chill in the refrigerator for 30 minutes, then bake blind for 10 minutes in a preheated oven, 375°F/190°C. Remove the beans and paper and return to the oven for 5 minutes.

3 Mash the squash and mix it with half the cream, season with salt and pepper, then spread it in the tart shell. Slice the cheese and lay it on top. Whisk the remaining cream with the eggs and egg yolk and pour the mixture into the tart pan, making sure it settles evenly. Arrange the sage leaves on the surface. Bake for 30–35 minutes and leave for 10 minutes in the pan before serving.

artichoke & pancetta tartlets

ingredients

serves 6

butter, for greasing

9 oz/250 g ready-made pie dough, thawed if frozen

all-purpose flour, for dusting

filling

5 tbsp heavy cream

4 tbsp bottled artichoke paste

salt and pepper

14 oz/400 g canned artichoke hearts, drained

12 thin-cut pancetta slices

arugula leaves

1¾ oz/50 g Parmesan or romano cheese

2 tbsp olive oil, for drizzling

method

1 Grease 6 x 3½-inch/9-cm loose-bottom fluted tartlet pans. Divide the pie dough into 6 pieces. On a lightly floured counter, roll each piece to fit the tartlet pans. Carefully fit each piece of dough into its pan and press well to fit. Roll the rolling pin over the pan to trim the excess dough. Cut 6 pieces of parchment paper and fit a piece into each tartlet, fill with dried beans, and let chill in the refrigerator for 30 minutes.

2 Bake the tartlet shells for 10 minutes in a preheated oven, 400°F/200°C, and then remove from the oven and take out the beans and parchment paper.

3 Meanwhile, stir the cream and the artichoke paste together and season well with salt and pepper. Divide among the tartlet shells, spreading out to cover the base of each tartlet. Cut each artichoke heart into 3 pieces and divide among the tartlets. Curl 2 slices of the pancetta into each tartlet and bake for 10 minutes.

4 To serve, top each tartlet with arugula, then, using a potato peeler, sprinkle shavings of the Parmesan cheese over the tartlets, drizzle with olive oil, and serve at once.

smoked salmon, dill & horseradish tartlets

ingredients

serves 6

butter, for greasing

9 oz/250 g ready-made pie dough, thawed if frozen

all-purpose flour, for dusting

filling

4 fl oz/125 ml/½ cup sour cream

1 tsp creamed horseradish

½ tsp lemon juice

1 tsp Spanish capers, chopped

salt and pepper

3 egg yolks

7 oz/200 g smoked salmon trimmings

bunch fresh dill, chopped

method

1 Grease 6 x 3½-inch/9-cm loose-bottom fluted tart pans. Divide the pie dough into 6 pieces. Roll each piece to fit the tart pans. Carefully fit each piece of dough in its shell and press well to fit the pan. Roll the rolling pin over the pan to trim the excess dough. Cut 6 pieces of parchment paper and fit a piece into each tart, fill with dried beans, and let chill in the refrigerator for 30 minutes.

2 Bake the tart shells for 10 minutes in a preheated oven, 400°F/200°C, and then remove the beans and parchment paper.

3 Meanwhile, put the sour cream, horseradish, lemon juice, capers, and salt and pepper into a bowl and mix well. Add the egg yolks, the smoked salmon, and the dill and carefully mix again. Divide this mixture between the tart shells and return to the oven for 10 minutes. Let cool in the pans for 5 minutes before serving.

feta & spinach tartlets

ingredients

serves 6

9 oz/250 g ready-made pie dough,
thawed if frozen

filling

8 oz/225 g/6 cups baby
spinach
2 tbsp butter
salt and pepper
5 fl oz/150 ml/²⁄₃ cup heavy
cream
3 egg yolks
4½ oz/125 g Feta cheese
1 oz/25 g/scant ⅓ cup
pine nuts
cherry tomatoes and sprigs of
flat-leaf parsley, to garnish

method

1 Grease 6 x 3½-inch/9-cm loose-bottom fluted tart pans.
Divide the pie dough into 6 pieces. Roll each piece to
fit the tart pans. Carefully fit each piece of dough in its
shell and press well to fit the pan. Roll the rolling pin
over the pan to trim the excess dough. Cut 6 pieces
of parchment paper and fit a piece into each tart, fill
with dried beans, and let chill in the refrigerator for
30 minutes.

2 Bake the tart shells for 10 minutes in a preheated
oven, 400°F/200°C, and then remove the beans and
parchment paper.

3 Blanch the spinach in boiling water for just 1 minute,
then drain, and press to squeeze all the water out.
Chop the spinach. Melt the butter in a skillet, add the
spinach, and cook gently to evaporate any remaining
liquid. Season well with salt and pepper. Stir in the
cream and egg yolks. Crumble the Feta and divide
between the tarts, top with the creamed spinach,
and bake for 10 minutes. Sprinkle the pine nuts over
the tartlets and cook for an additional 5 minutes.

4 Garnish with cherry tomatoes and sprigs of flat-leaf
parsley.

potato & pancetta muffins

ingredients

serves 12

1 tbsp sunflower or peanut oil,
    plus extra for oiling (if using)
3 shallots, finely chopped
12 oz/350 g/scant 2½ cups
    self-rising flour
1 tsp salt
1 lb/450 g potatoes, cooked
    and mashed
2 large eggs
12 fl oz/350 ml/1½ cups milk
4 fl oz/125 ml/½ cup sour cream
1 tbsp finely snipped
    fresh chives
5½ oz/150 g pancetta, broiled
    and crumbled into pieces
4 tbsp grated Cheddar cheese

method

1 Oil a 12-cup muffin pan with sunflower oil, or line it
    with 12 muffin paper liners. Heat the remaining oil in
    a skillet, add the chopped shallots, and cook, stirring,
    over low heat for 2 minutes. Remove from the heat
    and let cool.

2 Sift the flour and salt into a large mixing bowl. In a
    separate bowl, mix the potatoes, eggs, milk, sour
    cream, chives, and half of the pancetta together.
    Add the potato mixture to the flour mixture and
    then gently stir together until just combined. Do not
    overstir the batter—it is fine for it to be a little lumpy.

3 Divide the muffin batter evenly among the 12 cups
    in the muffin pan or the paper liners (they should be
    about two-thirds full). Sprinkle over the remaining
    pancetta, then sprinkle over the cheese. Transfer to a
    preheated oven, 400°F/200°C, and bake for 20 minutes,
    or until risen and golden. Remove the muffins from the
    oven and serve warm, or place them on a wire rack
    and let cool.

herb muffins with smoked cheese

ingredients

serves 12

1 tbsp sunflower or peanut oil, for oiling (if using)

10 oz/280 g/2 cups all-purpose flour

2 tsp baking powder

½ tsp baking soda

1 oz/25 g smoked hard cheese, grated

1¾ oz/50 g/scant ¾ cup fresh parsley, finely chopped

1 large egg, lightly beaten

10 fl oz/300 ml/1¼ cups thick strained plain yogurt

4 tbsp butter, melted

method

1 Oil a 12-cup muffin pan with sunflower oil, or line it with 12 muffin paper liners. Sift the flour, baking powder, and baking soda into a large mixing bowl. Add the smoked cheese and the parsley and mix together well.

2 In a separate bowl, lightly mix the egg, yogurt, and melted butter together. Add the yogurt mixture to the flour mixture and then gently stir together until just combined. Do not overstir the batter—it is fine for it to be a little lumpy.

3 Divide the muffin batter evenly among the 12 cups in the muffin pan or the paper liners (they should be about two-thirds full), then transfer to a preheated oven, 400°F/200°C. Bake for 20 minutes, or until risen and golden. Remove the muffins from the oven and serve warm, or place them on a wire rack and let cool.

soured cream muffins with chives

ingredients

serves 12

1 tbsp sunflower or peanut oil, for oiling (if using)
10 oz/280 g/2 cups all-purpose flour
2 tsp baking powder
½ tsp baking soda
1 oz/25 g Cheddar cheese, grated
1¼ oz/35 g fresh chives, finely snipped, plus extra to garnish
1 large egg, lightly beaten
7 fl oz/200 ml/scant 1 cup sour cream
3½ fl oz/100 ml/generous ⅓ cup plain unsweetened yogurt
4 tbsp butter, melted

method

1 Oil a 12-cup muffin pan with sunflower oil, or line it with 12 muffin paper liners. Sift the flour, baking powder, and baking soda into a large mixing bowl. Add the cheese and chives and mix together well.

2 In a separate bowl, lightly mix the egg, sour cream, yogurt, and melted butter together. Add the sour cream mixture to the flour mixture and then gently stir together until just combined. Do not overstir the batter—it is fine for it to be a little lumpy.

3 Divide the muffin batter evenly among the 12 cups in the muffin pan or the paper liners (they should be about two-thirds full). Sprinkle over the remaining snipped chives to garnish and transfer to a preheated oven, 400°F/200°C. Bake for 20 minutes, or until risen and golden. Remove the muffins from the oven and serve warm, or place them on a wire rack and let cool.

cheese & rosemary bites

ingredients

serves 40

8 oz/225 g cold butter, diced,
plus extra for greasing

9 oz/250 g/1¾ cups
all-purpose flour, plus
extra for dusting

9 oz/250 g/2½ cups grated
Gruyère cheese

½ tsp cayenne pepper

2 tsp finely chopped fresh
rosemary leaves

1 egg yolk, beaten with
1 tbsp water

method

1 Lightly grease 2 cookie sheets. Place the flour, butter, cheese, cayenne pepper, and chopped rosemary in a food processor. Pulse until the mixture forms a dough, adding a little cold water, if necessary, to bring the mixture together.

2 On a floured counter, roll out the dough to ¼-inch/ 5-mm thick. Stamp out shapes such as stars and hearts with 2½-inch/6-cm cutters.

3 Place the shapes on the prepared cookie sheets, then cover with plastic wrap and let chill in the refrigerator for 30 minutes, or until firm. Brush with the beaten egg yolk and bake in a preheated oven, 350°F/180°C, for 10 minutes, or until golden brown. Let cool on the cookie sheets for 2 minutes, then serve warm or transfer to wire racks to cool.

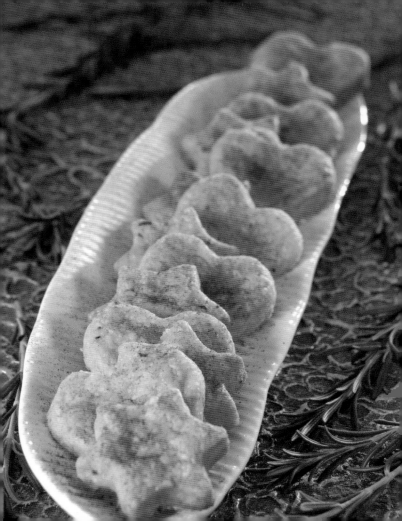

pesto palmiers

ingredients

serves 20

butter, for greasing
all-purpose flour, for dusting
9 oz/250 g ready-made
    puff pastry
3 tbsp green or red pesto
1 egg yolk, beaten with
    1 tbsp water
1 oz/25 g/¼ cup freshly grated
    Parmesan cheese
sprigs of fresh basil, to garnish

method

1 Grease a cookie sheet with a little butter. On a floured counter, roll out the pastry to a 14 x 6-inch/35 x 15-cm rectangle and trim the edges with a sharp knife. Spread the pesto evenly over the pastry. Roll up the ends tightly to meet in the center of the pastry.

2 Wrap in plastic wrap and let chill in the refrigerator for 20 minutes, until firm, then remove from the refrigerator and unwrap. Brush with the beaten egg yolk on all sides. Cut across into ½-inch/1-cm thick slices. Place the slices on the prepared cookie sheet.

3 Bake in a preheated oven, 400°F/200°C, for 10 minutes, or until crisp and golden. Remove from the oven and immediately sprinkle over the Parmesan cheese. Serve the palmiers warm or transfer to a wire rack and let cool to room temperature. Garnish with sprigs of fresh basil.

cheese straws

ingredients

serves 24

4 oz/115 g/generous ¾ cup
    all-purpose flour, plus extra
    for dusting
pinch of salt
1 tsp curry powder
2 oz/55 g butter, plus extra
    for greasing
2 oz/55 g/½ cup grated
    Cheddar cheese
1 egg, beaten
poppy and cumin seeds,
    for sprinkling

method

1 Sift the flour, salt, and curry powder into a bowl. Add the butter and rub in until the mixture resembles bread crumbs. Add the cheese and half the egg and mix to form a dough. Wrap in plastic wrap and chill in the refrigerator for 30 minutes.

2 Lightly grease several cookie sheets. On a floured counter, roll out the dough to ¼-inch/5-mm thick. Cut into 3 x ½-inch/7.5 x 1-cm strips. Pinch the strips lightly along the sides and place on the prepared cookie sheets.

3 Brush the straws with the remaining egg and sprinkle half with poppy seeds and half with cumin seeds. Bake in a preheated oven, 400°F/200°C, for 10–15 minutes, or until golden. Transfer to wire racks to cool.

index